D0424985

The Quattrocento Dialogue

Harvard Studies in Comparative Literature
Founded by William Henry Schofield
35

The Quattrocento Dialogue

Classical Tradition and Humanist Innovation

David Marsh

HARVARD UNIVERSITY PRESS
Cambridge, Massachusetts
and London, England
1980

Printed in the United States of America

Library of Congress Cataloging in Publication Data
Marsh, David, 1950-
The quattrocento dialogue.

(Harvard studies in comparative literature; 35)
Includes bibliographical references and index.
1. Italian literature—15th century—History and criticism. 2. Dialogues, Italian—History and criticism. 3. Humanism in literature. 4. Cicero, Marcus Tullius—Influence. I. Title. II. Series.
PQ4075.M3 1980 850'.9'002 79-15625
ISBN 0-674-74115-3

To my parents
and to the memory of
Myron Gilmore

Acknowledgments

I CAN RECORD HERE my gratitude to only a few of the many persons who have aided me in writing this book, originally submitted as a doctoral dissertation to the Department of Comparative Literature at Harvard University. Primary thanks are due my advisory committee—Professors Dante Della Terza, Walter Kaiser, and the late Myron Gilmore—for their advice and encouragement. The recent death of Myron Gilmore, which was a great loss to Renaissance scholarship, especially saddened those who remember his personal warmth and generosity.

The burden of work on this book was accomplished during a Fulbright year in Florence, Italy, and during a subsequent fellowship year at Villa I Tatti in Florence, 1976-1978. I am grateful for the personal interest and attention displayed by the directors of those programs, Cipriana Scelba and Craig Hugh Smyth respectively. While in Florence, I received indispensable counsel from Riccardo Fubini and Salvatore Camporeale, as well as friendship and assistance from Edward Lee, Jr., rector of the American Church.

The entire dissertation was revised according to the sound strictures of Aldo Scaglione. The prose was also scrutinized by Lawrence Lane, whose patient and penetrating eye has spared the reader innumerable solecisms and opacities. Gloria Ramakus and Carole Stone assisted with their editorial and typing expertise. All translations are mine.

I owe a special debt of gratitude to the generosity and hospitality of Professor and Mrs. Harry Levin and Mrs. Dorothy Usher Wilson of Cambridge, Massachusetts, and of Countess Federica Piccolomini of Florence, Italy. Mr. Levin has been particularly gracious in fostering my work, and I wish to thank him doubly for his personal and academic attentions. My greatest debt is owed, quite naturally, to my parents, Mr. and Mrs. Edward R. Marsh, without whose care and devotion this work would have been impossible.

Contents

The Quattrocento Dialogue

I

Cicero and the Humanist Dialogue

Let everyone follow his own belief, for, as you know, there is an immense variety of opinions and freedom of judgment.—Petrarch, *Secretum*

THE DEBATES and discussions of the early Italian Renaissance are vividly recorded in the philosophical dialogues of the Quattrocento humanists. Inspired by the writings of Cicero, these humanist dialogues examine philosophical questions in a contemporary setting. The evolution of the genre in the Quattrocento accordingly illustrates the development of emerging modern thought.

The Quattrocento revival of Ciceronian forms and ideals of dialogue represents the culmination of a literary and intellectual tradition which from antiquity to the Italian Renaissance was repeatedly transformed. The tradition begins with Cicero, the orator and eclectic philosopher who perfected the Latin dialogue in the first century B.C., and it ends with the Italian humanists of the fifteenth century, who sought to return to the Ciceronian concept of dialogue and discussion. During the Middle Ages two major figures shape decisively the course of the tradition. The first, St. Augustine, marks the end of the classical Ciceronian dialogue in the fourth century, and the second, Petrarch, initiates the dialogue's revival in the fourteenth century. As historical consciousness deepens in the early fifteenth century, the earlier representatives of the Latin intellectual tradition become the protagonists in a dramatic confrontation enacted and resolved in the dialogues of the Quattrocento humanists.

The neo-Ciceronian dialogue developed with particular rapidity and coherence during the first third of the Quattrocento in the writings of four humanists: Leonardo Bruni, Poggio Bracciolini, Lorenzo Valla, and Leon Battista Alberti. Bruni and Alberti embody the humanism peculiar to Florence in the early Quattrocento, and their dialogues examine secular problems by adopting the model of Cicero's *De oratore*. Poggio and Valla reflect more directly their experience in the Roman Curia, and their dialogues address questions of religion and ecclesiastical authority. Although all four writers treat moral problems, Bruni and Alberti seek to establish continuity with the secular culture of Trecento Florence, whereas Poggio and Valla break openly with the medieval doctrines and institutions of the Roman Church. At the end of the Quattrocento, the dialogues of Giovanni Pontano in Naples provide a synthesis of Quattrocento themes and Ciceronian ideals which closes the most vigorous phase of the humanist dialogue in the Italian Renaissance.

The origins of the dialogue as a literary form can be traced to Greece in the fifth century B.C., and it flourished during the following century in the philosophical writings of Xenophon, Plato, and Aristotle. The Greek word *dialogos* connotes an investigative discussion—as distinct from a simple conversation, or *logos*—among a number of persons. Contrary to what was thought in the Middle Ages, it is not limited to two people. The first dialogues of Xenophon and Plato portray the conversational inquiries of their mentor Socrates. The dialogues of Aristotle, intended for a wider audience than his extant treatises, survive only in fragments; hence the knowledge of them is deduced largely from the method of his imitator, Cicero. Typically, at this first stage of the genre's development, a topic is discussed in a historical setting, usually the Athens of Socrates' day, and a single speaker of superior logical and rhetorical talents, often Socrates, dominates the discussion.[1]

When three centuries later Cicero wrote a series of dialogues in order to introduce Greek philosophy to a Roman audience, he followed the Aristotelian model as a literary form suited to the exposition and examination of established doctrines. The derivative character of the Latin dialogue, originating in Cicero, persists through the Middle Ages and the Renaissance. Cicero's dialogues, which were destined to dominate the subsequent Latin tradition, provided an eloquent model for the rhetorical method of presenting arguments on both sides of a question, *in utramque partem disserere*, as the basis for discussing traditional philosophical doctrines.[2]

Cicero himself is indebted to Socrates, whose singular contribution to philosophy lay in the investigation of ethical questions. In his

Tusculanae disputationes, Cicero asserts that Socrates was the first to bring philosophical speculation back to earth, preferring moral problems to scientific and metaphysical questions (V, 4, 10). The moral emphasis of Cicero's dialogues reflects the practical orientation of Roman culture which, in seeking ethical guidance, looked to exemplary deeds and civic experience rather than to the abstractions of Greek treatises. Indeed, Cicero's choice of the dialogue as a means of exposition reveals his insistence on the historical precedents and the eminent personalities of Rome in the examination of practical questions. The Ciceronian dialogue, by presenting a discussion within a contemporary setting and portraying celebrated men as the interlocutors, makes frequent appeal to the lessons of Roman experience.[3] Just as the humble similes in Plato recall Socrates' discussions with Athenian craftsmen, Cicero's political perspective reflects the author's own experience as orator and statesman. In Cicero's greatest dialogue, *De oratore,* the value of Greek rhetorical precepts is constantly tested by the touchstone of Roman civic experience.

Cicero's education, like nearly all classical education, consisted of rhetorical training, that is, preparation for a career as an orator. This training, more than any philosophical allegiance, determined the constitution of Ciceronian dialogue. As a philosopher, Cicero often professed adherence to Academic skepticism, which left him free to choose among the possible arguments those that were useful in pleading his case. As long as education continued to emphasize rhetorical skills as a preparation for oratory, the Ciceronian mode of balanced arguments *in utramque partem* dominated the Latin philosophical dialogue.

Such education, and with it much of classical culture, ended with the collapse of Roman civilization and the rise of Christianity as the prevalent cultural force in the West. At this turning point in Western civilization, the personality and writings of Augustine are decisive for the history of the Latin dialogue. Augustine's conversion from classical philosophy to the Christian faith moved him to reject rhetoric and to substitute scriptural exegesis as the basis of education; the result was the death of the classical dialogue. Inspired originally by Cicero's dialogue *Hortensius,* Augustine had turned in his youth to the study of philosophy and successively investigated the doctrines of various sects before being finally converted to Christianity. His four dialogues of Cassiciacum—*De ordine, Contra Academicos, De beata vita,* and *Soliloquia*—which were written shortly before his baptism in 386, imply a condemnation of Cicero's Academic argument, transforming the classical dialogue's social inquiry for truth into an introspective search for God. For Augustine as Christian convert, the authority of Scripture obviated the necessity of discussion, and revealed truth clearly forbade as pernicious the ambiguous practice of arguing two sides of a question. The tranquil examination of one's own conscience in soliloquy was now the highest form of dialogue.[4]

The spirit of eclecticism and practical argument inherent in the classical Latin dialogue died with Augustine's conversion, to be replaced by the abstract symbolisms of the medieval dialogue, which often assumed the form of a timeless catechism. Together with Boethius' *Consolation of Philosophy* (c. 522), in which the allegorical discussion enjoins man's abnegation of the world, Augustine's soliloquies set the pattern for the dialogue of the early Middle Ages. Later, Scholasticism transformed the genre into a rigorously logical instrument of theological dialectic.

Nearly a thousand years after Augustine's conversion and his condemnation of the Ciceronian dialogue, the spirit, if not the form, of ancient dialogue was revived by Petrarch in his *Secretum* (1347-1353), a soliloquy-like interchange between the author's literary self and his Augustinian conscience. The return to the classical model evidently could not bypass the Church Father who had previously barred the way, and Petrarch openly confronts the obstacles posed by the figure of Augustine. Similarly, later humanists, such as Poggio and Valla, would engage Augustine indirectly in the covert polemics of their dialogues. Augustine had been converted and baptized at Milan, where he wrote his last classicizing dialogues depicting his sojourn at Cassiciacum. Seeking something like Augustine's conversion, Petrarch completed his *Secretum*, the first modern dialogue, at Milan as a colloquy between himself and the Church Father.

Although the *Secretum* asserts a return to the Ciceronian ideals of free discussion, it is closely bound to medieval forms of thought and expression, and its timeless setting lacks the social and historical dimensions essential to the humanist dialogue. Breaking away from the medieval models of Augustinian soliloquy, Boethian consolation, and Scholastic disputation, the Quattrocento dialogue emerges in 1401 with the first volume of Bruni's *Dialogi ad Petrum Histrum*, a work that announces, with programmatic explicitness, its indebtedness to Ciceronian notions of discussion. The novelty of Bruni's conception is emphasized by comparison with Trecento works such as Dante's *Questio*, Albertino Mussato's allegorical debates, and Petrarch's *De remediis*, or with the contemporary *De felicitate*, written in 1400 by the Paduan Francesco Zabarella. Bruni's *Dialogus I* expounds a program of Ciceronian themes by means of a discussion held in the circle of Coluccio Salutati in Florence at the beginning of the Quattrocento. At the outset of the work, the aged chancellor Salutati invokes the Ciceronian notion of *disputatio* as a free discussion rather than a Scholastic dispute. Bruni, in composing the second book of his *Dialogi* a few years later, introduced further Ciceronian elements in imitation of *De oratore*, thereby establishing a new ambiguity in the dialogue, the discrepancy between historical reality and literary fiction in the classicizing portrayal of discussion.

After Bruni's revival of Ciceronian forms and ideals, the Quattrocento dialogue enjoys remarkable diffusion and diversity. In the first half of the century the Ciceronian model adopted by Bruni is continued and elaborated by three humanists—Poggio, Valla, and Alberti—who were employed, as Bruni had been, in the Roman Curia. Fostered by the spirit of lively discussion found in the Roman Curia around 1430, the early phase of the Quattrocento dialogue exploits the new humanist enthusiasm for debate in examining moral questions, and it establishes the Ciceronian model adopted by Bruni as the dominant tradition.[5] In the second half of the century the Ciceronian tradition—represented by such humanists as Platina, Campano, and Landino—no longer shares the spirit of controversy and paradox characteristic of the first phase.[6] The philological erudition of Pico, Barbaro, and Politian had little use for the ambiguities of the dialogue form.

A number of humanists, including Alberti in his Latin works, imitated the model of Lucian, the Greek author of satirical and mythological dialogues; others followed various Greek traditions now accessible either in the original or in Latin translation. A synthesis of Quattrocento traditions both Greek and Latin is provided late in the century by the dialogues of the Neapolitan humanist Pontano, in which the academic classicism of later humanism begins to emerge. With the beginning of the sixteenth century, the humanist dialogue moves north of the Alps in the *Colloquies* of Erasmus, who was clearly influenced by Pontano, while the vernacular (*volgare*) dialogues of the Cinquecento in Italy, such as Pietro Bembo's *Asolani* and Baldassare Castiglione's *Courtier*, restore to the discussion the civilizing influence of women, who had been rigorously excluded from the humanist circles of the Quattrocento.

During the century between Bruni's first dialogue (1401) and Pontano's last (*Aegidius*, 1501), Italian humanists revived the Ciceronian model and fused that model with various elements of other traditions. Although Cicero's example predominates, three subsidiary traditions of dialogue reflect the influence exerted by Greek authors. The models for these traditions are the Socratic dialogues of Plato, the dialogue symposia of Xenophon and other writers (both Greek and Latin), and the comic dialogues of Lucian.

Although many humanists undertook translations of Plato's writings, few imitated the technique of Platonic dialogue.[7] Whereas Plato presents his arguments in dramatic rather than narrative form and never appears in his own works, most Quattrocento dialogues, except those of Lucianic inspiration, are introduced and narrated by the author, who often takes part in the conversation. Apart from such purely formal distinctions, Plato's early Socratic dialogues, with their singular concentration of argument and inquiry, found surprisingly few imitators in the Quattrocento. Yet in the first half of the century, three Latin works reveal the central influence of Socratic inquiry— Alberti's *Pontifex* (1437) and Valla's *De libero arbitrio* (1439) and *De professione religiosorum* (1442).[8] In their dramatic presentation of investigative argument dominated by the agile mind of a Socratic thinker, who in Valla's work is the author himself, these dialogues closely reproduce the form and spirit of Plato's Socratic inquiries. Alberti's *Pontifex*, a discussion between two Alberti bishops, seeks to define the duty (*munus*) of the episcopal office by comparisons with domestic and military obligations. Valla's *De libero arbitrio*, which relates a conversation between Antonio Glarea and Valla on the age-old problem of reconciling man's free will and God's prescience, ends with the inconclusiveness of Plato's early dialogues. Reminiscent of Alberti's *Pontifex*, Valla's *De professione religiosorum* compares, in a debate between Valla and an anonymous friar, the relative claims to salvation of lay virtue and sacred vows. In the Socratic inquiries of Alberti and Valla, it is no coincidence that the ecclesiastical profession is called in question. Their challenge of the clergy recalls the impugnment of the Sophists by Plato's Socrates: both the radical assertions of the Sophists and the conservative dogmatism of the church provoke the mordant criticisms of individual skepticism.

A second classical tradition of dialogue imitated in the Quattrocento follows the model of the *Symposia* of Xenophon and Plato. In late antiquity this tradition developed the symposiac dialogue as a forum for antiquarian lore in works of Plutarch, Aulus Gellius, Athenaeus, and Macrobius.[9] During the Quattrocento the symposiac tradition flourished in the Italian courts, where erudite dialogues paid tribute to the cultivation of the ruler and his adherents. Francesco Filelfo's *Convivia mediolanensia* (1440) depicts learned banquet discussions in Viscontean Milan, and Angelo Decembrio's *Politia litteraria* (c. 1460) celebrates the erudition of Leonello d'Este and his mentor Guarino Veronese at the court of Ferrara.[10] Poggio's *Historia con-*

vivialis (1450), a postprandial discussion of three learned questions, recalls Plutarch's *Quaestiones conviviales* but treats questions in the manner of Cicero's arguments *in utramque partem*. Reminiscent of the symposiac tradition as well are the depictions of the Neapolitan Academy in the later dialogues of Pontano, especially his *Actius* (1495-1499) and *Aegidius* (1501). Yet these works manifest a Ciceronian concern for moral questions as well as a delight in mere erudition, and their preference for contemporary experience rather than antiquarian learning distinguishes them from the other symposiac dialogues of the Quattrocento.

A third classical tradition of dialogue was the conscious blend of comedy and dialogue developed by the Greek writer Lucian in the second century.[11] It inspired Quattrocento humanists to compose their most novel kind of dialogues, in which they often sought to express moral indignation satirically in dramatic allegories and apologues. Such neo-Lucianic works typically present a brief encounter, or series of brief encounters, between a cynical and astute protagonist and one or a number of passers-by, often mythological figures or historical persons. In the first half of the century the principal representatives of this tradition are Alberti and Maffeo Vegio.[12] Alberti's *Intercoenales* (1430-1440) is a collection of short dialogues and fables which usually present gods and allegorical figures in discussion; his *Momus* (1443) is an extended fable, mostly in dialogue, of the vicissitudes of the god of mockery in mediating conflicts between heaven and earth. In Vegio's *Philalethes* the allegorical figure of Truth describes to her devotee Philalethes her mistreatment on earth, which recalls the similar account of Philosophia in Lucian's *Fugitivi*. Vegio's *De felicitate et miseria* presents the Lucianic ferryman Charon and the Virgilian helmsman Palinurus in an underworld discussion of mortal fortunes.

At the end of the century the neo-Lucianic dialogue is represented at the court of Ferrara by Pandolfo Collenuccio and at Naples by Antonio Galateo and Pontano.[13] Collenuccio's *Apologi quattuor* (c. 1499) continues the tradition of Alberti's *Intercoenales*, while his *Filotimo* and *Specchio d'Esopo* (1497) introduce the Lucianic tradition in the vernacular. Galateo's *Eremita* (1496) depicts the soul of a hermit as a cynic, similar to the Cyniscus of Lucian's *Jupiter confutatus*, who cross-examines various Biblical figures, Evangelists, and church founders in a spirit of irreverence. Pontano's first dialogue, *Charon* (1467-1470), combines in a underworld setting scenes of Lucianic satire and Ciceronian discussion. Pontano's *Antonius* (1482-1490), in which the Neapolitan circle discusses the life and thought of the late Antonio

Beccadelli, is marked by an alternation between the frenzied world and the tranquil academy, which recalls Lucian's blend of comedy and dialogue. Pontano's dialogue *Asinus* (1488-1492) abandons the realm of philosophical discussion altogether in a fantastic comedy reminiscent of Aristophanes. Pontano's last two dialogues, *Actius* and *Aegidius,* which portray an ideal humanist academy under the spiritual tutelage of the aged author, contain few comic elements. The *Aegidius* forms Pontano's literary testament, chronologically and thematically closing the era of the Quattrocento dialogue.

These three traditions—Platonic, symposiac, and Lucianic—complement the Ciceronian tradition of the humanist dialogue, and elements of all of them appear in the work of Poggio, Valla, Alberti, and Pontano. Yet the dialogues of Cicero had the greatest influence on the humanist dialogues which provide the most telling evidence of the intellectual innovations of the Quattrocento humanists. Cicero's dialogues present rhetorical examinations of traditional doctrines in a historical setting. Unlike Platonic dialogues, they are derivative and eclectic; unlike symposiac dialogues, they are concerned primarily with ethical questions; and unlike Lucianic dialogues, they portray serious discussions in historical settings. The dialogues of Cicero present philosophical inquiry in the framework of a leisured retreat; the interlocutors are cultivated men of affairs for whom discussion complements activity. In most of Cicero's philosophical works, the interlocutors are Cicero himself and his contemporaries, whose experiences and convictions are faithfully depicted. In the elaborate *De oratore* and *De republica* as well as in the essaylike *De senectute* and *De amicitia,* Cicero chooses interlocutors from earlier generations in order to lend authority to the discussion—the authority of Roman civic experience and moral dignity, not that of Greek erudition and culture.

The Latin word *humanitas* denotes both general culture and individual moral quality, and Cicero's dialogues are humanistic because they demonstrate the inseparability of the individual's learning from his role in society. Since the aim of the discussion is moral edification, the Ciceronian dialogue seeks to persuade rather than to dictate, and the method of inquiry is accordingly subjective and rhetorical rather than objective and dogmatic. Often younger Romans are present in the discussion, and the rhetorical character of discourse is determined by the educational concern of the interlocutors with the intellectual and ethical formation of future generations. Yet didacticism never precludes the freedom of the individual to choose, a freedom which reflects Cicero's own Academic skepticism and which is essential to the rhetorical and persuasive constitution of Ciceronian dialogue.

The spirit of Ciceronian dialogue was revived by Italian humanists in a conscious attempt to return to the ideal freedoms of Roman discussion and to break out of the confines of medieval thought created, at least in part, by the Augustinian condemnation of Academic argument. Petrarch's *Secretum* reasserts the methodological freedom of Ciceronian eclecticism through the words of his interlocutor Augustinus, and with Bruni's *Dialogi* the formal thematic imitation of Cicero is established as the dominant model for Poggio, Valla, Alberti, and Pontano.

While a close investigation of the Quattrocento dialogue confirms the predominance of Cicero as a model, it also indicates the complexity of Ciceronian influence, for the stylistic and structural model of Cicero's dialogues was adopted by Quattrocento humanists with significant modifications. The even tone and balanced arguments of Cicero's interlocutors, for example, are succeeded in the Quattrocento by more marked contrasts between personalities and by a freer pattern of argument. The clarity of Ciceronian terminology and historical setting is replaced by ambiguities of vocabulary and by ironies of character necessitated by the repressive climate of fifteenth-century Italy.

Cicero contributed signally to the method of the humanist dialogue, which strove to restore the Academic custom of arguing both sides of a question, *in utramque partem disserere.* Augustine's condemnation of this practice and his consequent rejection of the classical dialogue added a new complexity to the humanist revival of Ciceronian ideals of discussion. This revival often involved a covert confrontation of Augustinian authority and of the subsequent medieval tradition. Whereas Cicero for the Middle Ages was above all an authority (*auctor*) to be consulted and cited for his valuable sayings, for the humanists he was an eclectic philosopher-orator, free to examine and argue numerous philosophical questions.

In his dialogues Cicero had portrayed the polite learning, *humanitas,* of cultivated Roman contemporaries and their forebears, and it was this social and historical dimension of his dialogues that appealed to the humanists' sense of erudite fellowship and to their awareness of historical mission in reviving ancient ideals. The Ciceronian model clearly influenced the Quattrocento depiction of leisurely discussion between learned men who were prominent in public and private affairs. From Bruni to Pontano speculative discussion complements active participation in the business of the world beyond the humanist circle. As preparation for future activity and as instruction for moral betterment, the humanist dialogue often begins, like Cicero's *De oratore,* with an exhortation by a distinguished interlocutor, whose ideal discourse raises questions to be examined in the subsequent discussion. Thus, in Bruni's *Dialogi,* Salutati's praise of *disputatio* leads to a new evaluation of the Trecento poets Dante, Petrarch, and Boccaccio. Alberti's *Libri della Famiglia* begin with Lorenzo Alberti's moral injunctions, which occasion disagreement between Adovardo and Lionardo. In Poggio's *De avaritia* and Pontano's *Aegidius,* the sermons of Fra Bernardino and Giles of Viterbo inaugurate discussions of contemporary morality and eloquence.

The form of the Quattrocento debate tends to establish a polarity of opinion less clearly presented than the balanced oppositions of Cicero's philosophical arguments *in utramque partem.* In this respect the humanist dialogues of the Quattrocento resemble the freer pattern of *De oratore,* in which the first book is articulated by the contrast between Crassus and Antonius. In Bruni's *Dialogi* and in Alberti's *Libri della Famiglia,* two initially conflicting interlocutors move of their own accord toward a reconciliation which demonstrates their *humanitas.* Bruni's Niccoli is reconciled to Salutati and "restored" to the group by his recantation. In Alberti's *Libri della Famiglia* successive differences of opinion and temperament—Adovardo and Lionardo in Book I, Lionardo and Battista in Book II, Adovardo and Giannozzo in Book III—are resolved in familial affection and human understanding at the end of each book.

The affinities of Bruni and Alberti as authors of secular Florentine dialogues are clear. Their religious and Roman counterparts, the dialogues of Poggio and Valla which originated in the Papal Curia, reveal a greater complexity than the simple imitation of *De oratore.* In Poggio's *De avaritia* and Valla's *De vero falsoque bono,* the initial polarity between two speakers is superseded and adjudicated by an arbiter of higher dignity and authority. This development of the Ciceronian debate *in utramque partem* betrays the influence of the Augustinian model of *Contra Academicos,* adapted for the new purpose of exalting humanist values in the ostensible guise of theological conformity. Just as the initial debate requires the excuse of insincerity, so the final judgment assumes various outward tokens of Christian authority, such as a theological arbiter to pronounce definitive sentence on the debate. The addition of this Augustinian arbiter indicates the need of the Quattrocento dialogue to present an agreement acceptable both to the gathering itself and to the world at large. Instead of the skeptical suspension of judgment that closes Cicero's philosophical dialogues, the humanist dialogue tends to establish a final reconciliation. In Pontano's *Aegidius,* written at the start of the sixteenth century, the spirit of reconciliation pervades the discussion and seeks to harmonize the tensions inherent in diverse and discordant traditions, moving from Ciceronian eclecticism to humanist syncretism.

The resolution effected by the conclusions of humanist dialogues does not, however, establish an unchallengeable finality. Cicero's dialogues portray friendly, informal discussions in which philosophical questions arise and are examined in a leisurely setting, but in which moderation and politeness allow interruptions and postponements. The humanist dialogues of the Quattrocento demonstrate this same moderation, and the group often adjourns with an agreement to meet again and continue the discussion. Bruni's *Dialogi* end with Roberto Rossi's inviting the group to dinner on the following day, and the fourth book of Alberti's *Libri della Famiglia* ends with Adovardo's promise to address a further question the next day. Pontano's *Aegidius* likewise concludes with the promise of Suardino and Peto to attend the Academy sessions every day. The open nature of these discussions reflects the authors' appeal to their readers to continue and improve the arguments set forth. In Poggio and Pontano especially, the dialogue initiates a discussion to be carried on by readers of the work, expressing a notion of intellectual progress derived from Cicero's survey of the arts in his *Brutus*.

The most significant feature of the Quattrocento humanist dialogue is its revival of the Ciceronian principles of Academic argument and rhetorical freedom which are essential to an unbiased inquiry. Subordinating rhetoric to philosophy and philosophy to theology, Augustine had condemned Academic freedom and Ciceronian eclecticism in his dialogue *Contra Academicos*, which places reason in the service of scriptural authority and effectively reduces dialogue to the didactic and absolute catechism of his *Soliloquies*. Paradoxically, it is through the Augustinus of Petrarch's soliloquy-like *Secretum* that the autonomy of individual opinion is asserted. From Bruni through Poggio to Valla the rejection of abstract authority is couched in Cicero's paradigmatic deprecation of Pythagorean allegiance (*De natura deorum*, I, 5, 10), now invoked against the Aristotelian dogmatism of ignorant Schoolmen. Within humanist dialogues the group often mocks or isolates dogmatic rigidity, represented in the person of an intractably "Stoic" interlocutor out of touch with practical realities. In Bruni's *Dialogi* the fierce classicism of Niccoli must be tempered before the group reinstates him. In Valla's *De vero falsoque bono* Catone Sacco is goaded by the witty Maffeo Vegio for his rejection of man's natural condition. At the end of Book I of Alberti's *Libri della Famiglia* Adovardo entreats the magniloquent Lionardo not to play the Stoic with him. Even in Pontano's *Aegidius* the only dogmatic interlocutor, Chariteo, a recent convert to Hermetic doctrine who is prepared to swear allegiance to his new-found creed, is the object of the jests of Pontano and Pardo.

By contrast, the most vital interlocutors are the most controversial and the most flexible speakers in the group. As in Cicero, those who fully exercise the possibilities of rhetorical freedom often profess to speak more to stimulate others than to express their own opinions, and even today Poggio's Antonio Loschi and Valla's Maffeo Vegio are able to provoke readers. The classical exemplar of this controversial freedom was the Academic philosopher Carneades, whose arguments for and against justice symbolize the extreme freedom possible in secular debate. Condemned by Augustine and the subsequent Christian tradition, Carneades is rehabilitated by Valla's "Epicurean" Vegio as an ideal practitioner of the rhetorical freedom asserted by Cicero and formulated by Quintilian. The freedom of each to maintain and defend his own opinion, already asserted in Petrarch's *Secretum*, makes possible a debate in which the individual's reason no longer must yield to traditional authority. Unhindered by ideological and theological fetters, humanist discussion brings all aspects of a question into the open and examines conflicting arguments in the search for truth.

The rational nature of humanist argument rejects the dogmatic citation of authorities; the subjective nature of the debate is also accepted according to the rhetorical concept of argument as persuasion. Orators can persuade only by appealing to the psychological bent of their auditors and by adducing concrete proofs which are cogent because they are drawn from daily experience. Borrowing Cicero's metaphor, both Poggio and Valla insist that philosophy itself must weigh its arguments in the balance of common sense. Valla and Pontano establish the important principle that philosophical thought is based on the concrete significance of language and that reason itself must consult usage. Cicero had praised Socrates for bringing philosophy back down to earth (*Tusc. disp.*, V, 4, 10). The humanists of the Quattrocento reversed the Augustinian ascent from concrete realities to eternal abstractions by retracing the steps from theology to philosophy to rhetoric.

Whereas Augustine in the *Soliloquies* counsels and practices introspective debate as the highest form of inquiry, humanist dialogue restores the social basis of discussion, reviving the Ciceronian notion that men are spurred on (*incendere* "inflamed") by competitive debate. Humanist discussion is part of the individual's formation, an essential preparation for activity which supplements the solitary exercise of reading and study. At the same time, the beneficial effects of discussion are not merely intellectual but also moral. If the mind requires the exercise of debate, the soul desires eloquent persuasion for its moral edification. The rhetorical nature of humanist dialogue reflects its goal of ethical persuasion. This sense is clear in Poggio's *De avaritia,* which undertakes the discussion as a means of employing leisure hours for moral improvement; and it is strongest in Alberti's *volgare* dialogues, which seek to educate and edify the author's kinsmen and a wider Italian readership, especially the young.

The ethical concerns of the humanist dialogue require a rhetorical mode of persuasion and instruction, but they also require a new examination of traditional moral teachings in the light of recent experience. Reason and authority are tested against experience in Petrarch's *Secretum,* and the conclusion of Bruni's *Dialogi* integrates humanist discussion with the collective experience and consensus of the public. Poggio and Valla examine arguments according to the general practice of the day (*communis usus*), a realist criterion at odds with the "Stoic" idealism of traditional authorities. The theological invocation of God is replaced by an appeal to nature, and the precedent advanced is not what is divinely ordained but what occurs or exists naturally. The dialogues of Alberti depict the collective experience of his family and reflect the author's own vacillating attitude toward practical affairs. In Pontano's *Aegidius,* the assertion of universal belief in the soul's immortality and the linguistic appeal to common usage are simply complementary aspects of the acceptance and exaltation of what is natural, which for Pontano is also divine.

The attempt to reconcile recent experience with traditional doctrine may not always reach harmonious accord, and the humanist dialogue rejects a rigid categorization of the world according to fixed and transcendental systems like Scholasticism. The freedom of belief in discussion is matched by a freedom of organization. Methodological freedom requires formal freedom. The dialogues of Bruni, Poggio, and Valla exhibit a variety in the presentation of arguments which is inconceivable in Cicero's balanced discourses *in utramque partem* or in the rigorous syllogisms of Scholastic *sic-et-non* disputations. Alberti and Pontano employ the dialogue in a more discursive exposition, insisting that their interlocutors enjoy a freedom of organization.

This freedom precludes strict and absolute systems of thought, and humanist dialogues present their discussions not as definitive treatments but rather as bases for further examination of the subjects discussed. The relativity of knowledge means that succeeding generations must examine for themselves the validity of traditional doctrines. Thus a vivid sense of both history and progress is displayed in the humanist dialogue, which often retraces the development, and decline, of Western letters and thought from antiquity. Bruni's *Dialogi* are concerned with the historical value of Dante, Petrarch, and Boccaccio, thereby offering a necessary Quattrocento re-evaluation of Trecento culture. In Poggio the sense of progress derives from Cicero's notion of progress in the arts as formulated in his *Brutus*; and Alberti, who cites the same work in his treatise on painting, expresses the concept of creative succession in the visual metaphor of the mosaic floor. By the same token Poggio's prefaces express the author's conviction that his treatment of moral topics such as nobility is new. Alberti repeatedly notes the absence or insufficiency of classical discussions on contemporary problems. This awareness of novelty is found in Valla as well, for Antonio in *De vero falsoque bono* strives to deliver a new panegyric on celestial delights (*dicere nova conabor*). Pontano's dialogues likewise attempt to provide discussion of subjects not treated by classical authors and to lay the foundation for future study; even grammatical problems contribute to Pontano's Latin philosophy.

The relativity of the Quattrocento dialogue is a result of the conflict between traditional doctrines and contemporary experience. No longer suited to the novel patterns of modern life, traditional doctrines are presented in a new and freer organization, and contemporary experience is often transmuted or disguised by the indirect presentation of the dialogue form. Whereas the social and historical setting has an immediate bearing on the nature of the discussion, it is often subtly obscured by the use of classicizing terminology (*Stoici, philosophi*) or by allusions to classical authors, such as Boethius and Macrobius, which disguise the contemporary objects of polemical attacks. On the one hand, the Quattrocento dialogue engages in open polemics with past and present figures and institutions. Indeed, in the next century Erasmus would marvel at the unrestrained satire against the church found in the dialogues of Poggio and Pontano.[14] On the other hand, many of the polemics of humanist dialogue are merely hinted at or are couched in classicizing language that obscures their true targets.

Unlike the Ciceronian model, the humanist dialogue intentionally seeks to create ambiguities, such as discrepancies between historical figures and their literary portrayal, unorthodox interpretations of traditional authorities, and elusively shifting modes of argument which demonstrate both the range of rhetorical inquiry and the instability of traditional criteria. The purpose of such ambiguities is often to protect the author or his circle of friends: as late as Galileo's day, the threat of ecclesiastical authority recommended the dialogue form for treating potentially dangerous topics.

Such hidden polemics reflect the caution of the humanists, who exploited the form of the dialogue in order to avoid recriminations and reprisals from contemporary authorities. The humanist circles portrayed in Quattrocento dialogues are generally separated from a potentially hostile world beyond. Bruni's *Dialogi* express the fear of retaliation from the citizenry of Florence. Despite Poggio's frequent direct attacks on the clergy, his dialogues often confess the need for passing over delicate subjects. Valla's attack on "Stoicism" in the *De vero falsoque bono* serves as a paradigm of the humanists' use of classical labels to disguise a number of targets. When Valla attacks Boethius, he is also attacking the Scholastics. And when Pontano attacks Macrobius in *Antonius,* he in turn is attacking Valla.

The tensions caused by such overt and covert polemics—which, are far removed from the polite gatherings of Cicero's dialogues—demand resolution, and the humanist dialogue tends to have the interlocutors agree on an acceptable conclusion, usually a synthetic compromise of the positions advanced earlier in the discussion. Such harmonious conclusions satisfy a literary sense of resolution, and they also reflect the practical motive of the author's prudence: accused of dangerous or heretical teachings, the dialogue writer could point to the ostensible orthodoxy of his conclusion.

Perhaps the most striking resolution is that which effectively closes the era of the Italian humanist dialogue, the lofty syncretism of Pontano's *Aegidius.* Reconciling Aristotle, Cicero, and Augustine in a placid and elevated discussion, Pontano demonstrates the tendency of the late Quattrocento to syncretic philosophy and academic classicism. Ficino and Pico, his contemporary creators of philosophical systems, have little use for the dialogue form, since the new influx of diverse philosophical traditions can no longer be confined to the simple polarities of the Ciceronian dialogue. The philological classicism of Pontano's Latin philosophy tends to eliminate the immediacy and urgency of the humanist dialogue, substituting for the earlier passion for debate a new ideal of tranquil eloquence. The contact with contemporary experience which nurtured the early humanist dialogue repeatedly appealed to concrete practice, whereas the academic circle of the late Quattrocento begins to cite the correct usage of classical authors often far removed from contemporary realities. The Latin dialogue maintains its necessary contact with quotidian experience in the late Quattrocento only in the satirical depictions of the neo-Lucianic tradition. In the early sixteenth century, only an exceptional genius like Erasmus, for whom Latin was a living language, could preserve the connection between spoken and written word which makes the dialogue a vital form of expression. The future of the dialogue lay, quite logically, in the realm of the vernacular, and the dialogues of the Cinquecento deal from the outset with the problems of the *volgare* and its proper role in a new and emerging culture.

Petrarch's *Secretum* marks the beginning of the revival of classical dialogue by breaking with the dogmatism of the medieval dialogue and by asserting the Ciceronian notion of free discussion.[15] The *Secretum* presents a dramatic exchange between Petrarch's literary self, "Franciscus," and his depiction of Augustine, "Augustinus," in a symbolic confrontation between the author's awakening modernity and the Church Father's condemnation of the classical dialogue.[16] The work comprises three books of successive conversations between Franciscus and Augustinus with Truth standing by as a silent witness. In the first book Augustinus reproaches Franciscus for failing to contemplate his mortality, since meditation on death is the best remedy for his anguish. In Book II Augustinus examines Franciscus' conscience according to the medieval scheme of the seven deadly sins. In Book III, Franciscus defends himself against Augustinus' accusation that he is bound by the earthly chains of his love of Laura and his love of glory. The dialogue ends without achieving a reconciliation between the two interlocutors.

Petrarch's title, *Secretum,* indicates that his work is like a soliloquy, which Augustine in fact considered the highest form of dialogue. The opening scene of the *Secretum* presents the timeless setting of an internal debate like that of Augustine's *Soliloquies* or Boethius' *Consolation of Philosophy.* Recalling especially the initial encounter between Boethius and Philosophia in the *Consolation,* Petrarch's proem introduces Franciscus in troubled meditation when approached by a symbolic female figure, whom he recognizes as Truth (p. 22). But Franciscus' conversation with this abstract figure is not recounted. The dialogue begins only with the appearance of Augustinus, which shifts the level of discussion from the objective debate with Truth to the subjective psychological investigation with Augustinus, who has known human passions.[17]

With Truth as silent witness to the conversation, Augustinus leads Franciscus to a more secret and remote place, where they sit (p. 26: *in secretiorem loci partem . . . consedimus*). The scene suggests the influence of Augustine's *Confessions*, later invoked explicitly, and it adds a second sense to Petrarch's phrase, *secretum meum*, "my solitary retreat" (p. 26). In the eighth book of his *Confessions* Augustine used the same words, *secretum meum*, to describe his retreat with Alypius into the garden at Milan, where he was to hear the prophetic voice beneath the fig tree. In that passage too Augustine noted that the presence of Alypius did not disturb his solitude (*Conf.*, VIII, 8, 19): *Neque enim secretum meum non erat, ubi ille aderat.*[18] Petrarch's *Secretum* depicts a similar retreat during a spiritual crisis, a literary retreat (*secretum*), accompanied by the Church Father who himself overcame such a crisis.

Petrarch's proem establishes the similarity of the dialogue to Augustine's *Confessions* as a document of human experience when Truth hails the timely appearance of Augustinus:

> O Augustine dearer to me than a thousand, you know this devotee of yours, and you are aware how dangerous and prolonged a sickness has taken hold of him, who is closer to death in his illness because he is remote from recognizing his own disease. We must now care for this dying man's life, a task of affection which you may accomplish better than anyone. For he has always been deeply enamored of your name, and all teaching imbues the learner's mind more readily when imparted by a beloved teacher. If your present bliss has not caused you to forget your former miseries, you suffered much as he does while confined in the prison of your body. (p. 24)

The therapeutic aim of the dialogue, the diagnosis and cure of Franciscus' illness, is furthered by the affection which Augustinus inspires and by the similarity of his experience. The doctrine and counsel that Franciscus receives is not abstract but personal. Truth herself observes that the mortal Franciscus will more readily listen to the "human voice" of Augustinus (p. 26). Instead of attending to Truth as the magisterial voice of fixed, divine wisdom, Franciscus converses, and argues, with Augustinus, an interlocutor of comparable human experience and, as Truth calls him, "the best physician of passions he has himself known" (p. 24: *passionum expertarum curator optime*).

The *Secretum* is especially indebted to Augustine's *Confessions* as a record of human experience, and much of the dialogue suggests the model of a generalized confession, as shown in Book II where Franciscus is examined for each of the seven deadly sins. Yet Petrarch's *Secretum* is not the retrospective prayer of an obedient servant of God. Petrarch describes his dialogue as a "conversation with a friend" (p. 26: *familiare colloquium*) and says that his purpose in recording it is not to win personal glory but to enjoy repeatedly the sweetness, *dulcedo*, of the original exchange. Augustine's *Confessions* record a similar sweetness enjoyed by the author, but it is the sweetness of confession rather than of recollection (*Conf.*, II, 1, 1; cf. IX, 4, 7). In themselves, Augustine's memories are bitter; it is the act of worshipful obedience that is sweet. For Petrarch, on the contrary, the colloquy with Augustine is a social pleasure. Despite the anguish of his spiritual crisis, Petrarch characterizes his *Secretum* in much the same words as his epistles, the *Familiares*, which he calls a "sweet conversation" (*Fam.*, I, 1, 47: *dulce colloquium*). Petrarch's *Secretum* thus expresses the same social impulse more fully revealed in his letters.[19] When Bruni's *Dialogus I* appears half a century later, the affinities between dialogue and epistle are even more evident.

Introducing the *Secretum*, Petrarch notes that he has imitated Cicero and Plato by portraying the conversation dramatically without the narrative tags *inquam* and *inquit* (p. 26). This declaration, which becomes a commonplace of neoclassical dialogue technique, does not mean that the *Secretum* is modeled on the dialogues of Cicero or Plato.[20] The *Secretum* is closely bound to medieval tradition and portrays a symbolic debate in which, as Petrarch observes in the proem, the figure of Franciscus represents all mankind (p. 26).

The first book of the *Secretum* begins abruptly. Augustinus sharp reproaches erupt violently after the tranquil tone of the proem:

> *Aug.* What are you doing, wretched man? What do you dream? What do you hope for? Are you so unmindful of your miseries? Don't you remember your mortal state?
>
> *Fr.* Indeed I remember, and the thought always causes me to tremble. (p. 28)

This emotional tone establishes dramatically the topic for discussion and the often subjective nature of the debate. Each book of the *Secretum* moves from the dramatic portrayal of an emotional conflict to a logical inquiry concerning the emotions involved. In Book I, when Franciscus is chided by Augustinus, he at first blushes like a child; but when Augustinus maintains that no one is miserable against his own will, Franciscus ceases to blush, and a logical argument begins

(p. 32).[21] The voluntaristic thesis of Augustinus, which recalls the Stoic Thesis of Cicero's *Tusculanae disputationes*, Book V, forms the central topic of Book I and underlies all of the *Secretum*, returning at the end of Book III as the recurrent point of contention between Franciscus and Augustinus (p. 214).[22] This tension between reason and emotion is what makes the dialogue vivid.

In their logical examination of emotion, Franciscus and Augustinus say a good deal about their method of inquiry and establish important principles later adopted by the writers of Quattrocento dialogues. Although the *Secretum* contains many medieval features, such as the figure of Truth, its discussion is remarkably modern in tone and free from the dogmatism that is fatal to dialogue.[23] An exchange on the authority of Plato in Book II of the *Secretum* reveals Petrarch's subjective notion of psychological truth:

> *Fr.* I am well acquainted with the Platonic school you mention, both from your writings and from the accounts of other Platonic authors.
>
> *Aug.* It makes little difference from whom you have learned the truth, although authority is often helpful.
>
> *Fr.* For me Plato's authority is especially helpful, and I am deeply mindful of Cicero's remark in his *Tusculan Disputations.* "Even if Plato," he says, "adduced no reason (you see how I value him), he would still persuade me by his authority alone" . . . Authority and reason and experience so recommend Plato's opinion that I am sure there is no truer or holier utterance. (p. 100)[24]

Franciscus thus adds a third element, experience, to the Augustinian and Scholastic duality of authority and reason, and it is precisely this new criterion which determines the suitability of Augustinus as interlocutor.[25] For although the Church Father may represent impersonal authority, it is his similar experience which recommends him as a spiritual counselor, as Truth observes in the proem (p. 24). In Book I, for example, Augustinus appeals to the teachings of Franciscus' experience (p. 54: *experientia magistra*) to confirm his awareness of his own mortality.[26]

In Book II of the *Secretum* the truth of Plato's doctrine that the soul must be free from bodily desires is confirmed by the personal experience of Franciscus: "With God's help I arose and with a vast and incredible sweetness I perceived what was then good for me, and what had been harmful before. But having now fallen of my own weight back into my previous misery, I experience with bitter remorse what has undone me again. I have told you this lest you marvel that I profess having experienced this Platonic doctrine." When Franciscus adds that he has prayed to God for liberation from physical desires, Augustinus rebukes him, citing his own experience: "You did not pray with sufficient humility or temperance. You always kept a place for future desires; you always intended your prayers for a distant hour. I speak from experience: this happened to me as well. I used to say 'Grant me chastity, but not yet; delay a while'" (p. 100).[27] The canonical authority of Augustinus is thus complemented by the psychological verities of his personal experience. For Petrarch the temporal events of the *Confessions* are of greater moment than the timeless doctrines of Augustinian tracts and commentaries. Franciscus says that Augustine's *Confessions* seem to narrate his own story (p. 42); but when he cites Augustine's treatise *De vera religione,* he notes that the work was a departure from his usual philosophers and poets (p. 66).[28]

The separation of doctrine from experience renders invalid any system of teaching. Petrarch's *Secretum* establishes two themes common in the Quattrocento dialogue by calling in question both the rigidity of the Stoics and the abstraction of the Scholastics. Early in Book I, Franciscus characterizes the precepts of the Stoics as "contrary to popular beliefs and closer to truth than to practice" (p. 34: *populorum opinionibus aversa et veritati propinquiora quam usui*). Although he accepts Augustinus' denunciation of the masses as an unstable guide, Augustinus himself later observes about anger that the Stoic ideal of eradicating this passion may not be possible (p. 98). When Franciscus in turn marvels that few should know the school definition of man, Augustinus denounces the ignorance of the Scholastics (*dyalectici*), whose disputes are void of real understanding: "That endless verbosity of the Scholastics both abounds in catalogues of such definitions and glories in matters for interminable contentions, and yet they generally don't know the real meaning of what they say. Thus if you ask one of that breed about the definition of man or of anything else, you'll get a ready answer. But if you press further, there will be silence, and even if repeated argument has furnished a wealth of bold phrases, the speaker's behavior will demonstrate that he has no real conception of what he has defined" (p. 52). Augustinus' complaint is directed not so much against the discrepancy of words and things as against the failure of doctrine to correspond to morality. Scholastic speculation has detached human discourse from its proper sphere of experience and behavior. It is the task of the Quattrocento humanist dialogue to restore, and illustrate, the connection in ethical discussions.

The Augustinus of the *Secretum* thus challenges traditional authorities when their absolute truths become too far removed from the relative truths of experience. As an interlocutor in the dialogue, Augustinus even challenges his own authority—as Church Father rather than as human author of the *Confessions*—in encouraging Franciscus' search for truth. In a brief exchange between Franciscus and Augustinus, Petrarch establishes the freedom of the individual to express and defend openly his personal beliefs. Augustinus overturns the dogmatism of the historical Augustine which had effectively silenced the classical dialogue:

> *Fr.* I don't dare say that I think the opposite, for my estimation of you since my youth has grown so great that if I should hold any opinion other than yours, I may know that I have erred.
>
> *Aug.* Refrain from flattery, please. Rather, since I perceive that you have agreed with my words not so much from judgment as from awe, I grant you the freedom to say whatever you may think. (p. 36)

When Franciscus later asks Augustinus to proceed without fear of contradiction, Augustinus replies that argument is useful in seeking the truth, although one must not be quarrelsome:

> *Fr.* Since I have renounced all enthusiasm for contention, please proceed as you wish, for I am ready to follow, not oppose, you.
>
> *Aug.* I don't ask that. For if, as a learned man said, "truth is lost by quarreling too much," yet a moderate contention often leads to the truth. One should neither acquiesce to everyone without exception, as do those of a lazy and deadened wit, nor too eagerly dispute a patent truth, which is a clear sign of a quarrelsome mind.
>
> *Fr.* Very well, I approve and shall follow your advice. Proceed then. (p. 42)[29]

The promise of Franciscus in Book I to follow Augustinus' advice is fulfilled in Book III, where Franciscus defends his love for Laura as virtuous:

> *Fr.* While you may perhaps think the opposite, let everyone follow his own belief, for, as you know, there is an immense variety of opinions and freedom of judgment.
>
> *Aug.* In conflicting matters, there will be diverse opinions, but truth is always one and the same.
>
> *Fr.* I grant you that, but we are led astray because we stubbornly adhere to old opinions and are torn from them with difficulty. (p. 134)[30]

Franciscus thus recognizes the existence of transcendent truths; but since human beliefs vary, he asserts the right of everyone to maintain his own opinion. Again he appeals to Augustinus' personal experience ("as you know") and recalls the variety of opinions that the Church Father himself had held in his search for truth. Successively attracted by Manichean, Academic, Epicurean, and Neoplatonic doctrines, Augustine only gradually came to accept the Christian faith. Only by discussing such doctrines with friends and teachers and by shaking off his earlier beliefs did Augustine arrive at the truth, and the peace, of Christian teaching. As the Augustinus of the *Secretum* had previously recommended the utility of modest contention in seeking the truth, Franciscus now urges a clash of opinions which will shake adherence to traditional beliefs (*opiniones antiquae*) and bring the truth closer. From the *Confessions* rather than from the later treatises of Christian doctrine, Petrarch is familiar with the young Augustine's continual exploration of various philosophies, which demonstrated the validity of a sincere and soul-searching eclecticism. As Augustine himself records, his search for philosophical wisdom was inspired by reading Cicero's dialogue *Hortensius* (now lost), a work which exhorted him not to adhere to any single sect (*Conf.*, III, 4, 9). In the *Secretum*, Petrarch clearly anticipates the eclecticism of Quattrocento humanist dialogues.

The function of dialogue implicit in the *Secretum* lies in the confrontation of diverse viewpoints as a method for seeking higher truths. The obiter dicta of Franciscus and Augustinus formulate the principle of free inquiry which underlies the discussions of Quattrocento dialogues. To be sure, Petrarch's Augustinus insists on the existence of an eternal and unified truth, but this truth is not theologically conceived, and the figure of Truth stands as silent witness to the debate. In its occasional attacks on absolute dogmatism, the *Secretum* merely hints at the relative and multiple truths of later humanist dialogues. Yet despite the soliloquy-like character of Petrarch's "secret" debate, the mode and method of the work clearly prepare the way for the novel approach of humanist dialogues to the examination of traditional doctrines. The conflict of the *Secretum*, moreover, is psychological as well as ideological, and the difference of temperament between Franciscus and Augustinus, never finally reconciled, foreshadows the clashes of personalities in Quattrocento dialogues—between Bruni's Niccoli and Salutati, Valla's Catone and Vegio, and Alberti's Lionardo and Adovardo. The debate reflects the attitudes of the interlocutors as much as their philosophies.

In several respects, then, Petrarch's *Secretum* anticipates the relativity and freedom of discussion in Quattrocento humanist dialogues. Yet the structure of the work adheres to the pattern of instructive exchange represented in Christian dialogues from Augustine onward, and the Ciceronian model would not be adopted until two generations later by Petrarch's admirer Bruni. Because the *Secretum* deals with the introspective problems of Petrarch's spiritual crisis, it lacks the social dimension that was to shape the development of the Quattrocento dialogue. Even in this respect, however, Petrarch is a significant precursor of the social issues examined in humanist dialogues, because his epistolary collections, especially the *Familiares*, place the Trecento humanist in the larger context of his society and address contemporary questions that were to have profound echoes in Quattrocento dialogues. When at the beginning of the fifteen century Bruni's *Dialogi* inaugurate the Ciceronian imitation of the humanist dialogue, it is the social role of Petrarchan humanism which constitutes a central topic of discussion.

II

Leonardo Bruni and the Origin of Humanist Dialogue

What, by the immortal gods, could be of greater value than discussion in examining and investigating subtle questions? For in discussion, the topic is placed in the open and every aspect of it examined as if visually, so that nothing can escape our notice, nothing pass unseen, nothing deceive the gaze of all.

WITH THE *Dialogi ad Petrum Paulum Histrum* of Leonardo Bruni (1370-1444), the dialogue of the Quattrocento emerges full-blown from the Petrarchan antecedents of Senecan epistle and Augustinian soliloquy to assume the social and historical dimensions of the Ciceronian model.[1] Whereas Petrarch wrote to his contemporaries and to the ancients in a general moralizing style and employed the dialogue to dramatize the "secret" conflict of his personality and his Augustinian conscience, Bruni's *Dialogi* spring from the need to share with others the excitement of Florence, and the dialogue now portrays the vital tensions of a changing society. The more isolated and introspective debate of Petrarch's *Secretum* in part adopted the model of Cicero's anonymous exchanges in the *Tusculanae disputationes,* whereas the succession of generations and the civic spirit of interlocutors in Bruni's *Dialogi* recall the setting of Cicero's *De oratore,* a work that after Bruni was to dominate the Quattrocento concept of the dialogue form.[2]

Composed in 1401 and prefaced by a proem dedicated to the humanist Pier Paolo Vergerio, Bruni's *Dialogus I* recounts a discussion held in the house of the Florentine chancellor Coluccio Salutati during Easter of 1401. Present at the gathering are Salutati, Niccolò Niccoli, Roberto Rossi, and Bruni himself. Salutati begins the discussion by exhorting his young friends to practice the art of debating (*disputatio*), and he is answered by Niccoli, who objects that the present-day decline of letters makes learned argument impossible. Salutati replies that Niccoli's eloquence belies his point, citing the example of Dante, Petrarch, and Boccaccio as further evidence of the modern revival of letters. At the mention of the Trecento poets, Niccoli bursts into a tirade against their ignorance and the shortcomings of their works. Refusing to respond to these accusations, Salutati ends the discussion by reiterating his exhortation to debate.

In Bruni's *Dialogus II,* composed toward 1406, the group meets again on the following day in Roberto Rossi's gardens, where they are joined by Pietro di Ser Mino. Salutati begins the discussion by praising the beauty of the gardens and of Florence, and Pietro summarizes Bruni's recent *Laudatio*, a panegyric of the city. Salutati is asked to respond to Niccoli's attack against the Florentine poets, but he demurs, and it is decided that Niccoli himself should answer his charges of the day before. Niccoli now demonstrates the excellence of Dante, Petrarch, and Boccaccio, and the entire group welcomes his restoration to their opinion. The gathering ends as Rossi invites the group to dinner the following day.

Bruni's proem to *Dialogus I,* addressed to Vergerio, provides an epistolary introduction to the first dialogue and expresses the kind of personal sentiments that are characteristic of learned correspondence of the time, as in Bruni's own letters.[3] Having witnessed the misfortunes of his native Arezzo, Bruni consoles himself by the fact that he now lives in the most outstanding city of the age; and though separated from Vergerio in space, he feels joined to him in affection and through their letters (p. 44).[4] Bruni's personal sentiments for Vergerio are thus connected with his public pride in Florence, and he presents his dialogue as a means of sharing the advantages of Florentine culture with his absent friend. Vergerio had been greatly missed during a recent debate between Salutati and Niccoli; in order to permit him to enjoy the benefits of the learned circle at Florence, Bruni has recorded the debate and is sending it to the absent Vergerio.

The dialogue, then, in Bruni's earliest conception of it, grows out of an epistolary tradition. Providing a written extension of the humanist circle in Florence, the dialogue enables those not present to participate in the flourishing culture of Florence, where humanist studies grow daily and promise great benefits. Bruni's immediate purpose is to share a recent debate with a former member of Salutati's circle, but his more general aim is to communicate and demonstrate the superior culture of Florence to a wider Latin audience; hence a faithful rendering of the conversation will serve as the best evidence of Florentine eloquence.

Bruni's method in writing his *Dialogus I* is to strive for the utmost fidelity to the character of the participants. Vergerio himself, Bruni notes, may judge the result, since he is familiar with Salutati's distinctive gravity and Niccoli's verbal quickness and provocative manner. Such in fact are the characters of both speakers in *Dialogus I* from the outset, when Salutati assumes a customary expression of concentration (p. 46: *eo vultu quo solet cum quid paulo accuratius disturus est*). Despite Niccoli's virulent attacks on medieval ignorance and the shortcomings of Trecento culture, the Florentine chancellor preserves a dignified composure and refuses to be provoked. Bruni's fidelity to the character (*mos*) of the disputants also includes their respective positions in the debate of *Dialogus I,* as Hans Baron has observed.[5] Salutati's initial exhortation to the exercise of debate, for example, is corroborated as authentic by a letter of Bruni to Salutati in 1405, in which Salutati is cited as praising the power of debate to sharpen one's wits.[6] Historically accurate as well is Salutati's identification in the *Dialogus I* of Bruni's views with those of Niccoli.

While faithfully depicting the Florentine circle in 1401, *Dialogus I* nevertheless reflects the influence of Cicero's dialogues, especially the first book of *De oratore.* In both *De oratore* I and *Dialogus I,* a magisterial elder begins the discussion by encouraging the youths present to apply themselves to the pursuit of eloquence. Cicero's Crassus praises the accomplishments of the adolescents Sulpicius and Cotta in oratory and urges them to continue, while Bruni's Salutati reprimands the youths Bruni and Rossi, in contrast to the maturer Niccoli, for neglecting the important exercise of "disputation." In *De oratore* I, Crassus' initial praise of oratory elicits Scaevola's objections that orators do not found and preserve cities and that oratory does not embrace all the arts and sciences. Alluding to the major philosophical sects and to the liberal arts, Scaevola denies their contribution to the orator's art. In *Dialogus I* a similar objection is raised to Salutati's praise of debate by Niccoli, who complains that the present decadence of philosophy and the arts precludes the revival of learned debate (pp. 52-62).[8] Like Scaevola, Niccoli discusses the ancient philosophical sects and the liberal arts, but his viewpoint is in fact closer to that of Crassus when he insists on the connection between knowledge and eloquence. Attacking Dante and Petrarch later as inelegant and ignorant, Bruni's Niccoli borrows Crassus' repeated condemnations of ineptitude and impudence.[9]

In *De oratore* I, Crassus responds to Scaevola's objections that the art of oratory encompasses all other arts. His discourse in turn provokes Antonius, who denies the existence of such an art and ascribes true eloquence to philosophy, not rhetoric. Answering Niccoli's attack on present-day learning in *Dialogus I,* Salutati maintains that the study of extant classics makes learned debate possible, and he adduces the examples of Dante, Petrarch, and Boccaccio to demonstrate the achievements attained in the modern humanities. Provoked by the mention of the three Florentine poets, Niccoli explodes in condemnation of them and systematically impugns their accomplishments (pp. 68-74).[10]

Thus far the course of the discussion in *Dialogus I* follows the first book of *De oratore* both structurally and thematically. After the opening exhortations of the elder statesmen Crassus and Salutati, addressed primarily to the youngest members of the circle, a series of objections by maturer speakers—Scaevola and Antonius in Cicero, Niccoli in Bruni—leads indirectly to the central conflict of opinion: Crassus and Antonius differ concerning the status of oratory as an art, and Salutati and Niccoli clash in their evaluation of Trecento humanism. As these conflicts develop, both Crassus and Salutati hesitate to pursue the discussions they have initiated: Crassus is reluctant to continue "speaking about speaking" (I, 24, 112: *de dicendo dicere*), and Salutati wishes to cut short his "debate about debating" (p. 62: *de disputando disputatio*). Their reticence is partly an indication of modesty, but both cite their own experience in order to encourage the youths present to study assiduously and perfect their natural talent.[11]

Although the younger members of the circle welcome these long-awaited discourses, more mature speakers express reservations about the possibility of rhetorical excellence. In *De oratore,* first Scaevola and then Antonius raise objections to the assertions of Crassus, and the difference of opinion between Crassus and Antonius introduces and pervades their discussion of oratory. In *Dialogus I,* however, opposition to Salutati is concentrated in the person of Niccoli; and while the young Bruni and Rossi await the outcome of the incipient debate, Salutati—unlike Crassus—cuts short the discussion by promising a defense of the Trecento poets another time and by ironically reiterating his exhortation to practice debating (pp. 74-76).[12]

Until 1421, when a complete text was discovered at Lodi, Cicero's *De oratore* was available only in fragmentary versions according to three manuscript traditions.[13] In the most complete version of Book I, which Bruni seems to have known when writing *Dialogus I,* the text breaks off soon after Crassus has agreed to undertake a discussion of oratory for the benefit of Sulpicius and Cotta (I, 128); a subsequent fragment contains part of his praise of exercise, and most of a discourse on civil law (157-194).[14] From this text, the contrast with *Dialogus I* is apparent, for even if most of Crassus' and of Antonius' discourse is missing, the opening alternation of assertions and objections in *De oratore* I merely introduces the theoretical boundaries of the discussion to follow. In Bruni's *Dialogus I*, on the other hand, the abrupt confrontation of Niccoli and Salutati creates the same atmosphere of an introductory debate but remains unresolved. The lack of resolution is striking, both because Bruni fails to deliver his promised verdict—as Salutati fails to defend the Trecento poets—and because the dialogue obviously parallels the discussion undertaken by Crassus in *De oratore* I. The inconclusive nature of *Dialogus I* calls for a continuation or sequel in which the questions raised by Salutati and Niccoli find a satisfying response and resolution.

The formal expedient of Bruni's *Dialogus II*—the "recantation" of Niccoli and his re-evaluation of the Trecento poets—derives from the beginning of the second book of Cicero's *De oratore*, where Antonius modifies the position he had maintained the previous day against Crassus' assertion of an all-embracing "art" of oratory.[15] The feature of Niccoli's recantation was to become a commonplace of dialogue technique in the Quattrocento.[16] In both Cicero and Bruni, the setting of the second day changes to a colonnade (*porticus*), and new members join the circle—Catulus and Caesar in Cicero, Pietro in Bruni. The fact that the text of *De oratore* II available to Bruni was incomplete lends these minor details of setting a new significance. Bruni's *Dialogus II* begins abruptly, Salutati praising the beauty of Florence without mentioning the previous day's debate, and the presence of Pietro is not explained, although he has a good deal to say in the opening scene. If Bruni imitated the *De oratore* in the most complete text available, he would have found a model both for alluding to the discussion of the previous day and for explaining the presence of new interlocutors, because Crassus expresses discontent about his remarks of the day before, and Catulus and Caesar say that they have heard of the discussion and come to hear for themselves (II, 3, 13-14). But if Bruni was able to consult only the less complete text of *De oratore* II, which begins at 5, 19, where the newly arrived Catulus praises the setting as ideal for discussion, then the abrupt beginning of *Dialogus II* could be explained as an imitation of that more fragmentary version.

Like *Dialogus II*, the shorter version of *De oratore* II proceeds from a discussion of the group's setting to the resumption of the previous day's debate, in which the former dissenter recants. The introductory conversations in both works could scarcely be more different: in *De oratore* II, the *porticus* of Crassus' Tusculan villa suggests the topics of Greek philosophers and the leisure of Roman statesmen, while the beauty of the Florentine setting in *Dialogus II* calls to mind the patriotic sentiments of Bruni's *Laudatio* and the political greatness of the Florentines. Both conversations are soon cut short, however, in order to return to the problems left unresolved the day before, and Antonius and Niccoli begin their recantation.

Bruni's imitation of *De oratore* II is most apparent in the recantation of Niccoli in *Dialogus II*, where several Ciceronian passages are reproduced almost verbatim.[17] Both Antonius and Niccoli confess to having spoken with an ulterior motive: Antonius wished to shift the allegiance of Sulpicius and Cotta from Crassus to himself, and Niccoli hoped to persuade Rossi to sell his books.[18] On the first day, they did not express their real opinions, but now they are less contentious and expound views more acceptable to the group.[19] As a result, their overnight conversion is welcomed by a spokesman for the circle—Crassus in *De oratore* II and Rossi in *Dialogus II*. The same speakers, as hosts for continued discussion, invite the whole group by exacting a promise of their presence—Crassus for the same day, and Rossi for the next.[20] In Cicero's *De oratore* II, the arrival of Catulus and Caesar provides a credible pretext for Antonius' change of mind, and Antonius adds that Crassus himself spoke not his own opinion on the previous day but related what the Greeks taught (10, 41). Niccoli in turn echoes this statement, saying that he related only what he had heard from others (p. 94), but the context is ironic, for Niccoli has just finished defending Petrarch by citing the arguments of his Paduan devotees.

Whereas Antonius in *De oratore* II simply echoes the initial praise of oratory by Crassus and accepts his view that rhetoric is the source of eloquence, the recantation of Niccoli in *Dialogus II* is more complex. Niccoli's lengthy speech is imposed on him by Bruni's sentence, and he pleads his cause before Salutati as auditor and censor (p. 82). Unlike Antonius' complete agreement with Crassus, Niccoli's defense of the Trecento poets assumes a forensic aspect, which is later imitated in Valla's *De vero falsoque bono*. Niccoli begins with ethical proof of his cause, his own acts of devotion to Dante, Petrarch, and Boccaccio (p. 82). He has learned the *Divine Comedy* almost by heart, has traveled to Padua to obtain texts of Petrarch, and has adorned Boccaccio's library at his own expense: all these tokens of admiration for the Trecento poets will be recapitulated by Pietro at the end of Niccoli's defense (p. 96). Again describing his previous attack as a ploy to elicit Salutati's indignant response, Niccoli then proceeds to a defense of the Trecento poets (p. 84).

His defense of Dante is the longest and most elaborate, being divided in two parts. First, he defines the prerequisites of a poet as "imaginative art, stylistic elegance, and wide learning" (*fingendi ars, oris elegantia, multarumque rerum scientia*) and indicates the presence of all these elements in dante's *Divine Comedy* (pp. 84-86). Second, he replies to the charges he made the day before, attributing the egregious "errors" of the poem to poetic license rather than to Dante's ignorance. Niccoli's arguments are not wholly credible, for he glosses over Dante's bad Latin, citing his great popularity without reference to the demands of humanist learning (pp. 86-90).

Niccoli's defense of Petrarch continues his tendency to argue from public opinion rather than from personal standards: the arguments proving Petrarch's excellence are those Niccoli heard from Paduan friends of the poet, who insisted on his learning and versatility as a writer of both poetry and prose (p. 92). Concurring in their admiration, Niccoli expresses his own Florentine pride in Petrarch's accomplishments, which opened the way to humanist studies and won poetic laurels for the city of Florence.[21] Niccoli discounts his previous strictures on Petrarch's Latinity, explaining that revision of the *Africa* was prevented by the poet's death, and he repeats the dictum, originating with Salutati, that Petrarch surpassed Virgil in prose and Cicero in poetry.[22] Such is his answer to the arguments he advanced the previous day, which were not his own but borrowed from Petrarch's foolish detractors. Niccoli concludes with a terse encomium of Boccaccio, whom he earlier attacked, it would seem, for his role in promoting Dante and Petrarch.[23]

Having finished his defense of the Trecento poets, Niccoli urges Salutati to praise them as well, but the latter declines. Pietro in turn praises the speech as a proof both of Niccoli's devotion to the Trecento poets and of his excellence as a scholar. Niccoli replies that he recognizes his lack of greatness by comparison with the Trecento poets; returning to his pessimistic opinion of the age, which is the first objection he expressed in *Dialogus I*, he now says that he admires all the more the Florentine poets "who despite the obstacles of the age achieved a greatness equal or superior to the ancients by the abundance of their genius" (p. 96). Echoing Cicero's Crassus in *De oratore* I, Rossi hails Niccoli's conversion to the opinion of the group; and before the gathering disbands, he invites them all to dinner the following day (p. 98).

Several aspects of Niccoli's recantation are significant for the development of the Quattrocento dialogue. First is the neo-Ciceronian device of assuming a position to promote debate. Thus, in *De oratore* II, Antonius says that he must correct his previous remarks "by giving his own opinion rather than by contending" (10, 40: *non tam pug-*

nare . . . quam quid ipse sentiam dicere). Likewise, in *De finibus* I, Cicero speaks "to challenge Torquatus rather than to speak for himself". (7, 26: *magis ut illum provocarem quam ut ipse loquerer*). Similarly, the Niccoli of Bruni's *Dialogus II* claims to have spoken in order to arouse Salutati to praise the Trecento poets (p. 84). This rhetorical adoption of a position not one's own finds its most extreme and problematic example in the notorious case of Carneades' arguments for and against justice in the third book of Cicero's *De re publica,* no longer extant. Bruni would have known of the case from, among other sources, Lactantius' *Divinae institutiones*.[24]

A second aspect of Niccoli's recantation is not classical but rather reflects the limitations of free expression in Bruni's day. In an age in which unpopular or unorthodox opinions were subject to censure, a sort of moral immunity had to be provided for the speaker of an objectionable position. Beginning his attack of Petrarch in *Dialogus II,* Niccoli says that he will freely speak his mind but beseeches the group not to divulge his remarks (pp. 70-72: *Verum ego libere dicam quod sentio: vos autem rogo atque obsecro, ne hanc meam orationem efferatis*). Niccoli's request echoes the words of Crassus in *De oratore* I, but there is a clear difference between the security of Cicero's interlocutors and the insecurity of Niccoli, who fears an attack of the entire populace.[25] This tension is not resolved until Niccoli recants in *Dialogus II* and Salutati bids Rossi have the doors opened, "for we may now go forth without fear of calumny" (p. 96). The recantation effects Niccoli's restoration both to the circle of Salutati and to the Florentine public.

The recantation device has a third implication for the development of Quattrocento dialogue. The Niccoli of *Dialogus I* seems in fact to be the "true" Niccoli, for the views he advances in *Dialogus II* derive from other sources. For example, his later defense of Petrarch derives ostensibly from the Paduans but in fact from both Salutati and Bruni.[26] Yet within the dialogue, the Niccoli of the first day is renounced as insincere while the Niccoli of the second day professes to speak his true mind. *Dialogus II,* in short, undermines the historical accuracy of *Dialogus I.* This discrepancy between reality and fiction would not have escaped contemporaries who were acquainted with the personalities whom Bruni transforms for his own literary and ideological purposes. Bruni's effort to exculpate Niccoli by a fictitious recantation violates his original principle of historical accuracy, announced in the proem, and exploits the dialogue form for its very ambiguity. In dealing with controversial questions in an atmosphere of censorship such as that created by the Roman Curia, writers found that the ambiguities of belief and argument established by Bruni's *Dialogi* provided a model of considerable value. Thus when Poggio began to compose his first dialogue, *De avaritia,* he deliberately chose interlocutors whose characters belied their espoused views. After Bruni's *Dialogus II,* the way was open for the paradoxical and interchangeable selection of interlocutors in the Quattrocento dialogue. The freedom of speech within the dialogue could often be maintained only by dissociating the arguments advanced from the actual views of the interlocutors.

The freedom of discourse requisite to dialogue is already asserted by Bruni's *Dialogus I,* which begins programmatically with Salutati's exhortation to debate. Salutati's notion of *disputatio* is far removed from the Scholastic disputations of the day; Salutati himself is careful to provide a series of Ciceronian synonyms in order to distinguish his notion of discussion and debate from the conventions of medieval disputation. In his opening speech he describes his visits to Luigi Marsili and vaunts the wisdom he drew from "these debates or conversations, which I call disputations" (p. 50: *his sive disceptationibus sive collocutionibus, quas disputationes appello*). Similarly, in his response to Niccoli he defines his recommended exercise as "conversation, inquiry, and discussion of the objects of our studies, which in a single word I call disputation" (p. 66: *collocutio, perquisitio, agitatioque earum rerum quae in studiis nostris versantur: quam ego uno verbo disputationem appello*).

Such synonyms are necessary in order to restore to the word *disputatio* its classical meaning of philosophical discussion. Bruni's *Dialogus I* shows the influence of the classical "disputation" par excellence, Cicero's *Tusculanae disputationes*. In his initial praise of discussion, Salutati lauds the value of debate to refresh the mind: "If one's mind is tired and weak and generally shrinks from studies as a result of long inactivity and continuous reading, what could restore and refresh it more than conversations and discussions held in a circle or gathering, where one is greatly spurred on by glory, if he wins, or by shame, if he loses, to further reading and study?" (p. 40). The notion of being "spurred on by glory" (*gloria incendi,* literally "inflamed") echoes Cicero's dictum in the first book of *Tusculanae disputationes* that "honor nourishes the arts, and all are spurred on to their studies by glory" (2, 4: *honos alit artes, omnesque incenduntur ad studia gloria*). The social ideal of discussion represented by Cicero's dialogues was rejected by Augustine in his *Soliloquies*, and it is only with Bruni's *Dialogi* that the Ciceronian ideal is reinstated in the new spirit of humanism.[27] The bold endorsement of glory as a human motivation, formulated in *Dialogus I* by Salutati, is more clearly an expression of Bruni's generation than of Salutati's, and it marks a decisive step beyond the struggle of Petrarch's *Secretum*.[28]

Also derived from Cicero, and from the same preface to the *Tusculanae disputationes*, is the historical concept of philosophy expounded by Niccoli in *Dialogus I*. Niccoli effectively confirms Salutati's description of the competitive origins of philosophical investigation:

> Let us take philosophy, then, to consider that art above all which is the mother of all the fine arts, and from whose source our humanities are entirely drawn. Philosophy was once brought from Greece to Italy by Cicero and replenished by the golden stream of his eloquence; in his books the whole basis of philosophy was set forth, and the separate schools explained. In my opinion, his work contributed greatly to spurring on the studies of various men, for as each began to study philosophy, he chose at once a sect to follow and learned not only to defend his own opinion but to refute that of others. Hence arose the Stoics, the Academics, and the Peripatetics, and the Epicureans, and hence arose all the contentions and disagreements between them. (p. 54)

Like Cicero, Niccoli maintains that all the arts and sciences are interconnected, and he associates the flourishing of Latin letters in Cicero's day with the diffusion of learning.[29] But his Ciceronian ideals serve only to foster his virulent pessimism, and he attacks medieval authors and thinkers as both inelegant and ignorant. The misuse made of Aristotelian texts by Scholastic philosophers is condemned in particular, and here again the underlying arguments advanced by Niccoli derive both explicitly and implicitly from Cicero. In denouncing the Schoolmen's ignorance of Aristotle, Niccoli cites the testimony of Cicero's *Topica* that even classical philosophers were seldom familiar with Aristotelian doctrines (p. 56).[30] He then proceeds to condemn the medieval versions of Aristotle in Latin because they contradict the ancient praise of Aristotle's eloquence (p. 58).

Niccoli is exasperated by the Scholastic abuse of citing Aristotle as an indisputable authority. His objection is twofold: the text of Aristotle cited by the Scholastics is the intolerably rough version of the medieval translators, and Aristotle's authority is regarded as the equivalent of sacrosanct truth which it is wrong to contradict:

> What egregious philosophers we have today, who teach what they do not know! . . . if asked on whose authority and precepts they depend in their remarkable wisdom, they reply "the Philosopher's." By this they mean

> Aristotle's. So if they must prove something, they cite a passage from these books which they say are Aristotle's—harsh, absurd, and confused words sufficient to annoy and weary anyone's ears. "Thus spoke the Philosopher," they say, whom it is forbidden to gainsay: with them "thus he spoke" (*ipse dixit*) is tantamount to the truth, as if he were the only philosopher, or his opinions as fixed as if the Pythian oracle of Apollo had uttered them from his holy shrine. (pp. 54-56)[31]

Niccoli's denunciation of the incontrovertibility of Aristotelian texts constitutes the methodological basis of the Quattrocento dialogue: discussion of the truth must not be impeded by hierarchies of authority. Aristotle is only one of a number of philosophers whose opinions and example may be cited. The secular and classical comparison with the oracle of Apollo at Delphi, here employed to deny the eternity of Aristotelian views, clearly divorces them from the theological systems of Scholasticism. Of paramount importance is the notion, fundamental to Quattrocento dialogue, that knowledge is not fixed eternally; historical context and the fluidity of debate both play a role in the search for truth. Niccoli's citation of the authoritative *ipse dixit* in this passage echoes Cicero's critique of the Pythagoreans in the proem to his *De natura deorum* I, a work Niccoli cites in asserting the interconnection between the arts and sciences. Cicero's critique reads:

> Those who seek to know what my opinion is on every topic seem more curious than is necessary, for in discussion (*in disputando*) we must seek the weight of reason rather than that of authority. Indeed, students are often hindered by the authority of those who profess to teach them, since they stop applying their own judgment and accept the judgments of someone they approve. Nor do I endorse the custom of the Pythagoreans, who, it is said, when asked why they asserted something in a discussion used to reply "thus he spoke"—"he" being Pythagoras. For them a preconceived opinion was so strong that authority was valid even without reason. (5, 10)[32]

This seminal passage, implicit in the words of Niccoli in *Dialogus I*, expresses Cicero's mistrust of authority as an impediment to discussion (*in disputando*); reliance on mere authority precludes rational investigation in debate. Cicero is not attacking the authority of Pythagoras, nor is Niccoli attacking Aristotle; rather, both object to the blind allegiance of their followers which silences debate. Bruni's Niccoli insists on the plurality and mutability of philosophical positions in asserting that Aristotle is neither unique nor his opinions fixed, and he thereby points the way for the writers of dialogue in the

Quattrocento, who cite both ancient and modern precepts and examples, sacred or profane, for their validity in argument, not for their authoritative value. The dialogue form in effect provides a subtle means of removing traditional texts and concepts from the context of rigid, authoritative systems in order to examine them in the shifting criteria of humanist discussion.

A related feature of the Quattrocento dialogue is established by Bruni's *Dialogi ad Petrum Histrum*, namely the presentation of discussion in its historical and social setting. This setting is defined in terms of both the humanist circle and the circle's relation to the outside world. In *Dialogus I*, Bruni's stated principle of faithful reportage entails historical fidelity. For example, he accurately depicts the conflict between the two generations of Salutati and Niccoli at the beginning of the fifteenth century in Florence. The aged Salutati refers to Dante, Petrarch, and Boccaccio as being extolled by universal consent (*consensu omnium*).[33] Salutati thus expresses his agreement with the society beyond the humanist circle, but young Niccoli's response reveals the historical tension between traditional society and the new humanist generation. Niccoli, who is unyielding in his rejection of medieval culture and Scholasticism, is positively violent in denouncing the opinions of the contemporary masses concerning the Trecento poets: "What Dantes, what Petrarchs, what Boccaccios do you cite to me? Do you think that I judge by the opinions of the masses, and approve or disapprove as the multitude itself? Far from it. When I praise something, I repeatedly insist that my reason be clear. I have always suspected the multitude, with good reason: their judgments are so corrupt that they create more ambiguity than certainty. Do not marvel, then, to learn that I have a different opinion from the populace about these triumvirs, as it were, of yours " (p. 68). Niccoli's contempt for popular opinion later becomes a notable feature in Poggio's dialogues, in which Niccoli's Stoic idealism consistently opposes the unstable opinions and realities of everyday life.

These internal and external tensions of the society portrayed in *Dialogus I* are resolved both artistically and artificially in *Dialogus II*—artistically in the Florentine civic spirit of the opening discussion, and artificially in the historically improbable recantation and reinstatement of Niccoli as a harmonious member of both the humanist circle and the Florentine public. In fact, the internal consensus of the group in *Dialogus II* is an innovation which conceals the polarities of *Dialogus I* by isolating Niccoli as the sole representative of the younger generation of militant classicists. This internal consensus, moreover, requires a modification of Salutati's views before the dissident

Niccoli can be restored by the device of recantation. Accordingly, on the judgment of Caesar, Salutati meets the young Bruni halfway (p. 78).[34] Both Salutati and Rossi invoke the will and judgment of the Florentine people in their discussion of Guelph victory (pp. 78-80), and Niccoli's recantation draws upon the testimony of popular esteem for the Trecento poets as confirmation of their greatness. Where in *Dialogus I* he removed Dante from the number of humanists and relegated him to the company of common laborers, Niccoli now says he did so in order to place Dante above the humanists as a source of delight to the entire population (p. 86: *universa civitas*).

Niccoli's recantation modifies the total rejection of medieval culture of *Dialogus I*. Although Niccoli previously condemned Dante for studying medieval quodlibets, he now adduces as evidence of Dante's Latinity his numerous disputations (p. 90: *qui totiens disputarit*), thereby restoring the medieval sense of the word *disputatio*, which Salutati had employed in a Ciceronian manner. Niccoli also praises Dante's *Comedy* because its formulations of Christian doctrine nearly surpass the acuteness of the theologians and philosophers "in their schools and leisure" (p. 86: *in scholis atque in otio*). This last phrase echoes Cicero's description in *Paradoxa Stoicorum* of the Stoics "in their schools and leisure" (3: *in gymnasiis et in otio*). Bruni's adaptation of the Ciceronian expression foreshadows the classicizing vocabulary of later humanist dialogues, especially those of Poggio and Valla, in which the words *philosophi* and *Stoici* imply the contemporary counterparts of theologians and dialecticians. Yet while Poggio and Valla often employ such terms to disguise the target of their polemics, Bruni makes clear the identity of the theologians rivaled by Dante. Like Alberti's *volgare* dialogues, Bruni's *Dialogi* are generally secular in argument and relatively free of the ecclesiastical tensions found in Poggio and Valla.

Bruni's device of the recantation creates the fictional illusion of a reconciliation between the humanist circle and the popular tradition of Florentine culture. At the end of the dialogue the chancellor Salutati symbolically calls for the opening of the doors, and the humanists leave the Rossi gardens to return to the city. The closed and divided circle of *Dialogus I*, now unified by the civic spirit of Bruni's *Laudatio*, opens into a larger unity of cultural ideals and historical awareness with Florentine society.

The interaction of humanist circle and Florentine society depicted in the *Dialogi ad Petrum Histrum* is remarkably un-Ciceronian. Cicero's dialogues portray the leisurely discussions of Roman statesmen as a recreation from the business of politics. Bruni has likewise chosen a holiday setting, Easter, but the interlocutors of his *Dialogi* are aware of an intimate connection of their discussion with Florentine society. The Florentine society implicit in the *Dialogi* is that of the merchant oligarchy. Niccoli's contemptuous relegation of Dante to the wool workers (*lanarii*) might have offended the powerful Wool Guild (p. 70). Indeed, the length of Niccoli's attack and defense of Dante indicates the extent of Dante's popularity in Florence, as has now been shown by Christian Bec, who also suggests that Petrarch was not widely read in Florence during the early Quattrocento.[35] In his recantation Niccoli asks whether the Florentines can remain indifferent to their fellow-citizens when they are so warmly praised by "foreigners," that is, by northern Italians (p. 94). Bruni clearly desires a rapprochement between the new classicism of humanist learning and the traditional culture of the merchant oligarchy and no doubt hopes that his *Dialogi* might serve to bring the two closer together, by urging the humanists not to reject Dante and the merchants not to neglect Petrarch. In the conclusion of the *Dialogi*, Bruni can at least envision such a harmonious reconciliation between old and new.

III

Poggio Bracciolini and the Moral Debate

I know you are afraid that someone whom you correctly judge may think himself offended, but all are allowed to speak the truth.

THE DIALOGUES OF Poggio Bracciolini (1380-1459) constitute the first modern example of the form used generically in an extended literary program.[1] Whereas humanist epistolary collections are common after the example of Petrarch, Poggio is the first to base his literary reputation on a series of dialogues rather than on his collected letters. To be sure, Poggio had already begun to collect his own letters when he wrote his first dialogue, *De avaritia,* in 1428, and the moralistic criticism of his dialogues merely elaborates the lively reportage of his epistles. Yet Poggio reserved the honor of first publication to his dialogue *De avaritia,* which he intended for a wider readership than his more outspoken epistles, and the work proved an immediate literary success.[2] Poggio's *De avaritia* provides a significant link between Bruni's *Dialogi ad Petrum Histrum* and Valla's *De vero falsoque bono,* and it also serves as a useful introduction to the themes and methods developed in Poggio's later dialogues.

The dialogue portrays the conversation of a gathering of secretaries from the Roman Curia, who have dined at the house of Bartolomeo da Montepulciano near St. John Lateran in Rome. The principal interlocutors are Bartolomeo, Antonio Loschi, Cincio Romano, and the theologian Andreas of Constantinople. The conversation begins after dinner with a discussion of the recent sermons of Fra Bernardino in Rome. Antonio praises the friar's eloquence and his power to move the people, but Cincio objects that, like other preachers of the day, Bernardino fails to cure the spiritual ills of his hearers. Bartolomeo concurs, noting that the greatest of these ills are lust and avarice, of which the latter is more pernicious and more widespread, being rarely condemned by the clergy. Antonio asks Bartolomeo to discourse on this important topic, and Bartolomeo accepts, on condition that Antonio shall succeed him in speaking (I, 2-5).

At this point, Andreas of Constantinople arrives and inquires about the nature of the discussion. The group is at first reduced to silence by his dignity and authority, but he begs that the discussion continue. In a three-part speech Bartolomeo undertakes the condemnation of avarice that he promised, first defining avarice, then demonstrating its destructive effects on human society, and finally denouncing its prevalence among old men. Antonio replies to Bartolomeo's discourse by returning to his initial comparison of lust and avarice, which extenuates the effects of avarice by contrast with those of lust, and then answers the several arguments of Bartolomeo's speech in order. He is succeeded by Andreas, who excuses Antonio's speech in defense of avarice as insincere and then responds to his arguments in order, occasionally interrupted by the polemical asides of Cincio. Andreas concludes with a lengthy peroration condemning avarice on the basis of scriptural and patristic texts, and all, including Antonio, welcome his beneficial homily. Night having fallen, the group breaks up (I, 6-31).

This simple, three-part debate on the moral topic of avarice follows in part the model of Ciceronian discussions *in utramque partem*, while the final role of Andreas reflects the influence of Augustine's Cassiciacum dialogues. As a neo-Ciceronian dialogue, *De avaritia* resembles Bruni's *Dialogi ad Petrum Histrum*. In both works an initial discussion concerning the benefits of discourse—Salutati's praise of disputation and the praise of Bernardino's sermons—leads to a denunciation of contemporary standards of eloquence: Bruni's Niccoli laments the decline of classical wisdom in Scholastic quibbles, and Poggio's interlocutors question the moral efficacy of the preachers of the day. These initial exchanges introduce the central debate in both works, involving opposing discourses based on the rhetorical antithesis of praise and blame.

In Bruni's *Dialogi*, the Niccoli of Book I attacks the reputation of Dante, Petrarch, and Boccaccio, while his recantation in Book II provides a defense and laudation of them. This antithesis is clearly formulated by Poggio when he summarizes the *Dialogi* in his funeral oration of 1444 for Bruni: "He published a very eloquent dialogue, in the first book of which he attacked the excellent and learned men Dante, Petrarch, and Boccaccio and their learning, eloquence and works; in the second book, their virtue is praised in defense of the first" (II, 668-669).

The same antithesis of attack and defense found in Bruni's *Dialogi* appears in the first two lengthy discourses on avarice in Poggio's dialogue. Discussing a first draft of the work in a letter of June 10, 1429, to Niccoli, Poggio describes his original choice of interlocutors: "I had assigned the first role of attacking avarice to Cincio, who is considered greedy, and the role of defending it to Antonio, who is rather prodigal. I had done that intentionally, so that a greedy man would attack avarice and a spendthrift defend it" (Ton., I, 278).[3] On Antonio Loschi's advice, Poggio had later substituted Bartolomeo for Cincio (Ton., I, 273), but he had clearly planned the antithetical debate as an argument between unlikely proponents and opponents of avarice. In part, this ethical irony was necessary to protect the integrity of the speaker defending avarice: thus Antonio, "who is something of a spendthrift, defends avarice, for the vice is more safely defended by someone far removed from it" (Ton., I, 273). But Poggio's use of this ethical irony also serves to reinforce the "rhetorical" aspect of the debate, for even in his revised version Poggio's first two interlocutors begin their discourses by admitting that they speak primarily to promote the discussion. Introducing his attack on avarice in words more suited to Cincio, Bartolomeo says that he will address the group not so much to speak his mind as to provoke Antonio or Andreas (I, 6). Similarly, Antonio prefaces his defense of avarice by invoking the Academic custom, condemned a thousand years before by Augustine, of arguing on both sides of a question, *in utramque partem:* "Following the custom of the Academics, who used to debate against what others said, I shall relate a view different from Bartolomeo's; you shall judge whether it is acceptable" (I, 6).

The conclusion of *De avaritia,* where Andreas denounces the vice, arrives at a general agreement such as that reached by Niccoli's recantation in Bruni's *Dialogus II*. In the latter work, Bruni himself imposes the sentence on Niccoli "to defend the same men whom he had attacked the previous day," to which Niccoli agrees, prefacing his defense of the Florentine poets with a personal excuse: "Above all be assured that I attacked them yesterday only to arouse Coluccio to praise them. But it proved difficult to make this most prudent of men think I had spoken sincerely and had not invented my view" (p. 82). In Poggio's *De avaritia,* Andreas likewise begins his attack on avarice by excusing the insincerity of Antonio's defense of the vice:

Besides, I think Antonio spoke not sincerely, but for some other reason . . . As we hear of someone who praised the immoral tyrant Dionysius of Sicily and blamed the pious Plato in order to exercise his eloquence, so I perceive that you, a very liberal man, undertook the defense of this vice which you knew should be condemned before all others. I'm sure that you have spoken not to excuse the vice, but to attack it, so that from your arguments I might have greater ability to refute what can be said in its favor and to expose the ugliness and baseness of this great evil. We know that you, Antonio, as a liberal man are far from any taint of avarice and even from any suspicion of it. (I, 17-18)[4]

Although this passage recalls Poggio's fear of slandering his contemporaries (Ton., I, 274), it also suggests the influence of Bruni's *Dialogi*. After Niccoli's condemnation of the *iniquitas temporum* in *Dialogus I*, Salutati responds that Niccoli has in fact confuted his own arguments: "I think that his elaborate speech served not so much to excuse him as to condemn him, for what he argued with words his speech disproved in fact and in truth" (p. 64).

More significant, however, is the affinity of this passage with Niccoli's recantation in *Dialogus II*, where Niccoli himself indicates the discrepancy between the insincerity of his attack upon the florentine poets and the reality of his devotion to them. By absolving Antonio from possible charges of avarice, Andreas prepares the way for the unanimity expressed at the conclusion of *De avaritia* where, as in Bruni, the formerly dissident speaker is restored to the consensus of the group, which may then adjourn without fear of public reproach:

Ant. I am glad that I argued in favor of the greedy, so that we could hear your remarks.

And. I only hope they were worthy of your hearing. And if you approve them, I have no reason to fear the judgment of others. But since we have conversed enough and night has fallen, I think we should go. (I, 31)

The design of Poggio's *De avaritia* nevertheless cannot be said to be directly modeled on the structure of Bruni's *Dialogi*, which had been written some twenty years earlier. Yet it is probable that Poggio was familiar with Bruni's work and found in it confirmation of his own concept of the dialogue according to the notion of arguing *in utramque partem* for the sake of discussion rather than from personal conviction. As a close friend of Niccoli, Poggio would have sensed the irony of Bruni's *Dialogi*, in which the true-to-life portrayal of Niccoli in Book I as a "sharp man quick in provoking," is discredited by the recantation of Book II.[5] The Niccoli of Poggio's later dialogues never changes his true-to-life position. Thus in *De avaritia* the initial debate between Bartolomeo, originally Cincio, and Antonio serves as a rhetorical exposition of the problems that are to be resolved by the third speaker, Andreas. Just as Niccoli's recantation leads from the debate of *Dialogus I* to the acceptable laudation of *Dialogus II*, so Andreas' exoneration of Antonio turns the dispute concerning avarice, which was originally to be argued by the unlikely opponents Cincio *contra* and Antonio *pro*, into an elevated homily denouncing avarice and praising virtue.

From the beginning Poggio had reserved to Andreas the task of condemning avarice definitively. Writing to Niccoli about his first draft of *De avaritia*, Poggio calls the work "a dialogue against the avaricious," and he discusses in the same letter the suitability of Andreas as an exponent of the Christian condemnation of avarice: "In the second place, avarice is attacked by Andreas of Constantinople, who as a religious man seemed a suitable person to answer Antonio and to use the authority of Holy Scripture in censuring the vice of avarice" (Ton., I, 272-273). The authority of Andreas is emphasized by his late entrance, when his friends allude, with a suggestion of antiecclesiastical irony, to his dignity as censor and theologian.[6] His discourse, which is as long as the whole debate between Bartolomeo and Antonio, supplies the verisimilitude missing in the preceding arguments by rejecting them as insincere (*non ex animi sententia*) and by responding with a Christian discourse appropriate to his character and office. Andreas' condemnation of avarice as the root of all evils constitutes the central moral lesson of the dialogue as Poggio describes it in the preface to his *Contra Hypocritas* of 1447 (II, 45); and the ample citations from St. John Chrysostom reflect Poggio's enthusiasm for patristic homilies, dating from his years in England (cf. Ton., I, 30-31). Having responded to the arguments of Bartolomeo and Antonio, Andreas delivers an exhortation against avarice not found in the sermons of contemporary preachers, thereby both resolving the debate and providing the moral benefits that were the purpose of the discussion.

This "Christian" resolution of the dialogue, in which a pious and authoritative figure dismisses the previous debate between two disputants of a classicizing bent, recalls the Cassiciacum dialogues of Augustine in general and the first book of his dialogue *Contra Academicos* in particular. In the latter work, which marks the end of the classical dialogue in antiquity, the youthful Licentius and Trygetius argue whether philosophers may ultimately know the truth. Their debate is interrupted by their teacher Augustine, who praises their skill in discussion but insists that he now act as arbiter between them (*PL*, 32, 918).[7] Christian authority thus pronounces sentence on a two-part classical debate. Augustine likewise intervenes in Books II and III to resolve the discussion for the moral and spiritual betterment of all (929, 941). Poggio's *De avaritia* follows this Augustinian pattern while asserting Ciceronian freedom in debate, but Poggio's use of Augustine in structure and theme constitutes a singularly un-Augustinian argument.

The three-part debate of the *De avaritia* examines various arguments concerning avarice in the speeches of Bartolomeo, Antonio, and Andreas. Bartolomeo and Antonio begin by comparing avarice and lust. Bartolomeo compares the moral effects of avarice and lust, applying the social standard that characterizes his discourse, and extenuates the effects of lust as being limited to the individual, while condemning avarice as injurious to all mankind (I, 4). Responding to Bartolomeo, Antonio reverses the criterion from social to individual—a reversal fundamental to his defense of avarice—and after adducing the deleterious effects of lust, he expounds the compatibility of avarice with qualities of excellence (I, 10-11).

Upon the arrival of Andreas, Bartolomeo begins his discussion in the traditional manner by defining the term *avaritia* according to the classical etymology *avidus aeris* ("greedy for bronze") found in Gellius and Isidorus (I, 6).[8] Antonio immediately takes exception to this archaic derivation, noting that "contemporaries are moved by a desire for gold and silver, not bronze" (I, 6: *Auri enim argentique nostri homines cupiditate ducuntur, non aeris*), and this insistence on contemporary realities sets the tone for his subsequent discourse (I, 14). Despite the humor of his objection, Antonio later takes full advantage of this neutral definition. Stripping the concept of avarice of all but an economic sense, he rapidly identifies avarice with the universal human motivations of gain and self-preservation:

> In the first place you said that the avaricious are so called because they are too desirous of bronze, gold, and silver, but if all those desirous of money are called avaricious, nearly everyone will be thought guilty in these terms. For we all undertake all our actions for the sake of money; we are all moved by a desire for profit—and great profit at that—and if you remove this desire, all business and work will cease entirely. Who would do anything with no hope for his own benefit? The larger the profit, the more readily we undertake an affair; all pursue and desire this profit. (I, 11)[9]

Having exploited this economic sense of avarice in order to prove its universality, Antonio boldly seizes on a definition given by none other than Augustine and argues that avarice is the basis of altruism:

> In his book *On Free Will*, the most learned of the Latin fathers, St. Augustine, wrote that avarice is wanting more than what is enough, a definition less weighty than yours. If he is right, we must admit that we are all avaricious by nature, for that which everyone desires must be regarded as derived from nature and arising by her influence. Indeed, you will find no one who does not desire more than what is enough, no one who does not want a large surplus for himself . . . One sows only to provide enough both for himself and for his family. Think what general confusion would result if we only wanted what was enough for ourselves. The practice of the most welcome public virtues, mercy and charity, would be eliminated, and no one could be either beneficent or generous. For who will give to another if he has no surplus to give? (I, 12-13)[10]

Responding to Antonio, Andreas corrects both his definition of avarice and his conclusion that avarice is a natural impulse. First, Andreas distinguishes between desire (*cupiditas*) and avarice (*avaritia*), which is merely a special type of desire. Since the desire to accumulate wealth is necessary to the preservation of life and to the performance of generous actions, it may be considered natural, provided it is only a moderate desire. Avarice, on the contrary, is immoderate. It also replaces man's natural independence—a notion derived from Cicero's *De officiis*, I, 4, 13—with an unnatural slavery to gain. Andreas restores to the discussion the moral implications of the notion of avarice, which had been eliminated by Antonio's economic use of Augustine's simple definition of avarice as wanting more than enough. Conceding the natural existence of moderate desire, Andreas observes that an excessive desire of gain conflicts with another natural impulse in man, his desire to remain free and even to dominate and excel others. But whoever is possessed by overwhelming greed subjects his will to the slavery of desire. Andreas thus accepts part of Antonio's argument—the existence of natural impulses in man—but indicates the ethical ideal of moderation as reconciling man's diverse natural impulses. As proof of the servitude of the greedy to their passion, Andreas cites a passage from Chrysostom, whom he subsequently quotes repeatedly, not for his theological position but for his persuasive formulations of the psychology of the avaricious. According to Chrysostom, the desire for money is more savage than a tyrant and subjects its victim to a slavery of the passions more bitter than servitude to a human master (I, 19).

Bartolomeo had proceeded from his definition to a twofold condemnation of avarice from a social perspective (I, 7-8): the greedy are both harmful to the general welfare (*communis utilitas*) and lacking in the virtues essential to social bonds (*amicitia et benivolentia*). Antonio at first responds to this general charge by identifying avarice with the simple accumulation of wealth. He says that money is necessary for the common needs of civil life and that Aristotle in his *Politics* regards money as a means of doing business and drawing up contracts. Thus, if one condemns this appetite, one must condemn the other appetites that nature has given mankind. By nature, Antonio continues, all people seek to preserve themselves, and money is the means of doing so (I, 12).[11]

Antonio identifies the avaricious with the rich and, with the contemporary evidence characteristic of Poggio's writings, praises the civic magnificence that rich men contribute to modern civilization. Money is necessary as a sort of lifeblood of the commonwealth; and since the avaricious abound in money, they must be deemed the basis and foundation of society: "For if the commonwealth should need help, would we turn to the poor merchants and those who profess to despise wealth, or to the rich, that is, to the avaricious (for without avarice money is seldom amassed)? Is it better for the city to be full of wealthy citizens, who can protect themselves and others with their wealth, or of the needy, who can aid neither themselves nor others?" Many who are considered avaricious nonetheless aid the commonwealth and exercise great civic authority, avarice being no hindrance to participation in public affairs: "In fact, the avaricious often contribute great ornaments and beauty to their cities. To omit ancient examples, how many magnificent houses, outstanding villas, churches, colonnades, and hospitals have been built in our day by the money of the avaricious: if it had not been for them, our cities would entirely lack their greatest and most beautiful ornaments!" (I, 15).[12]

Responding to Bartolomeo's charge that the avaricious are incapable of friendship and generosity, Antonio reverses his position: denying the importance of money in benevolence, he separates the notion of wealth from the alleged virtues of the avaricious. The central duty of friendship is concerned not with money but with obligations and benevolence, which Antonio thinks the greedy may practice since wealth plays only a small role in maintaining friendships (I, 16). Antonio continues this reversal when he returns to the problem of the general welfare; reversing the ideal standard of the common good (*communis utilitas*) to the practical reality of general usage (*communis usus*), Antonio states the economic principle that one man's profit is another man's loss. As for Bartolomeo's objection that the greedy forget the general good in an eagerness for their own, Antonio maintains that such is the custom of almost everyone, not just the greedy. Who really seeks the public good without regard to private gain? Speaking from experience, Antonio says that he has to the present day never known anyone who could safely neglect his own interest:

> The philosophers say a good deal about placing the common good (*communis utilitas*) first, assertions more specious than true. But we must not regulate our lives by the standards of philosophy. It is usual and accepted by general usage (*communis usus*), and indeed has been the practice since the world began, that our own affairs affect us more than public affairs. We must admit this fact unless we prefer to speak in lofty phrases rather than according to usage. Yet if you think avarice harmful because making money entails many people's losses, you must also detest commerce and any other activity which seeks to make a profit. For no profit can be made without someone's loss, since whatever one person gains is taken from another. (I, 16-17)[13]

In his response to Antonio, Andreas shifts the discussion back to the moral level of Bartolomeo's discourse. He deals first with the problem of friendship, a classical concept which he indentifies with Christian love. As in his proof that avarice is unnatural, he corroborates his opinion by citing Chrysostom's analysis of the psychology of the avaricious; the value of the citation, he adds, consists in an authority confirmed by reason itself (I, 24). Replying to Antonio's praise of the avaricious as contributors to the general welfare, Andreas denies *a priori* the compatibility of avarice with social virtues, again citing Chrysostom:

> Avarice is destructive of all good qualities: hear how it is described by Chrysostom, whose opinions I cull as from a fertile field. "Avarice," he says, "is a destructive thing which deadens both sight and hearing, making men more savage than beasts. It permits no thought of friendship, of society, or even of the soul's salvation, but like a fierce tyrant makes slaves of its captives and, what is worse, forces them to love the author of their slavery, causing incurable sickness at heart. Avarice has declared a thousand wars, filling the streets with blood and the cities with mourning." (I, 26)[14]

Bartolomeo's discourse ended with a condemnation of avarice in old men, his interpretation of Virgil's description of the Harpies providing a lengthy peroration probably intended to compete with the allegorical preaching of St. Bernardine himself (I, 8).[15] At the end of Bartolomeo's discourse, Antonio asserts that the avarice of old men is a result of their experience, not a contradiction of it. Realizing the value of money in combatting life's hardships, avaricious old men provide for themselves and their families by acquiring and accumulating wealth. Again assuming a pragmatic and pessimistic stance, Antonio blames the realities of "nature" for the necessity of heaping up riches:

> If you think the greed of old men a base thing, the fault lies not in the prudence of a man who prepares himself against unexpected and unforeseen events, but in the frailty of nature, which subjects us to so many tests, abandons us in so many exigencies, and surrounds us with so many difficulties, against which we must seek the support of wealth, unless we wish to philosophize idly about words rather than about realities. Consequently, it is certain that greed is not only natural to man but useful and necessary, since it teaches him to provide himself with the securest means known of enduring the frailty of human nature and of avoiding misfortune. (I, 17)[16]

The topic of avarice in old men invites Andreas' apparent conclusion. With an allusion to Plato's *Republic*, Andreas expresses the opinion that the avaricious should be banished from the ideal state. Bartolomeo assents, and Cincio formulates a law which Cicero himself had surprisingly omitted from his ideal republic: "Let there be no greedy men in the cities; let any such be expelled by public decree" (I, 27). With this consent established, Andreas proceeds to his final point, which he makes succinctly by citing Cicero's remark that he cannot understand the point of old men's greed, since nothing could be less prudent than to seek more provisions when the journey remaining is shorter.[17] This Ciceronian dictum merely restates the observation of Bartolomeo that old men have even less cause to be anxious about wealth since they have fewer years ahead (I, 8).

Andreas has now addressed the principal arguments of the discussion begun by Bartolomeo and Antonio. Yet instead of ending with the allusion to *De senectute*, Andreas pronounces moral judgment on avaricious old men. As a peroration, he delivers a Christian homily on avarice as the root of all evils, taking Paul as his text (I Tim. 6:10). Poggio later wrote to Niccoli that he was not entirely satisfied with the conclusion of his dialogue (Ton., I, 273); he may have been displeased by either the homiletic style or the mixture of classical and Christian elements. Yet Poggio drew upon an eminent humanist source for the peroration of Andreas, Petrarch's letter against the avarice of bishops

(*Fam.*, VI, 1), which foreshadows Poggio's antiecclesiastical diatribe, interspersing classical maxims with Biblical citations.

The peroration of Andreas identifies the Pauline *cupiditas* of the Vulgate with the *avaritia* he denounces, in order to preserve his previous distinction between cupidity and avarice while citing the Latin Bible. Antonio's statement that avarice is necessary is obviously not true, Andreas argues, for avarice is in fact useless and destructive; nothing could be more destructive than the source of all ills. Paul attests that all ills arise from avarice: his golden saying is that the root of all ills is cupidity, by which he means that from which avarice proceeds. In his peroration, Andreas treats the topic of avarice for the first time from a Christian viewpoint. The classical notion of friendship (*amicitia*) here becomes Pauline love (*charitas*), and the vice of avarice is now identified with idolatry and heresy according to passages from Paul and Augustine. To be sure, even here the import of Andreas' citations from the Church Fathers is not theological, for he wishes to encourage the humanists to translate Chrysostom into eloquent Latin, and in the conclusion he quotes both Plautus and Horace (I, 27-30). But after his classical reply to Antonio, Andreas' hortatory invocations of sin and damnation, addressed not to the *tu* of Stoic diatribe but to the *vos* of Paul's Epistles and Christian sermons, marks a shift to the eternal verities of religion.

The shift is not absolute, for classical expressions and concepts pervade the lessons drawn, and Christ and salvation are not mentioned in Andreas' stoicizing final words: "When you depart this life, riches will desert you, and you will go forth naked, poor, and abandoned, descending to the underworld to plead your cause without an advocate before that terrible judge who cannot be corrupted by gold. You will have no help, no protector, no defense, but that provided by virtue and good deeds." This classicizing tendency is affirmed in Bartolomeo's approbation of Andreas' discourse, where Lucian and Silius Italicus are cited to corroborate the classical notion of an underworld judgment in which worldly goods play no part. Andreas welcomes these citations, not as ancient authorities but as testimonies of the truth: "So they have written, and others have written much as well; yet these are not the voices of one man or another, but of nature and truth itself" (I, 30). Antonio adds his voice to the consensus of the group, who then adjourn.

The discussion thus arrives at a consensus confirmed by the opinions of great men who agree concerning the truth. In Poggio's dialogues, the truth emerges from rational examination of opinions and arguments, and transcends traditional values of authority and position. In *De avaritia,* for example, classical and Christian authorities are evaluated in the same manner. Antonio cites the testimony of Lucian that Aristotle and many other philosophers were avaricious; yet although their example would suffice to defend avarice by their authority alone, he proposes to set aside any question of authority and to examine the question rationally (I, 11). Andreas replies to the example of Aristotle's alleged avarice by discounting his possible moral failing and by insisting instead on his recognition of the truth: "nowhere in his works does he praise avarice, but places it rather among the vices, far removed from virtue; so that even if he were himself avaricious, he would still be compelled by the force of truth to declare avarice an evil" (I, 19).

The independence of truth from individual ethical limitations is reflected as well in Poggio's constitution of the initial debate *in utramque partem* between Bartolomeo (originally Cincio) and Antonio. While the defense of avarice requires an unlikely advocate in order to avoid recriminations, Poggio also chooses an unlikely interlocutor to denounce the vice, thereby implying that the validity of the arguments is independent of their exponents' characters. Similarly, the maxims (*sententiae*) of authorities both classical and ecclesiastical are cited for their suitability in the argument and for their consonance with reason; as Andreas says when the group reaches their rational agreement, "these are not the voices of one man or another, but of nature and of truth itself" (I, 30). Whereas Bruni's *Dialogi* created a sort of debate *in utramque partem* through the device of Niccoli's "recantation" and thereby removed the dialogue from the realm of historical fidelity, Poggio boldly announces his constitution of the dialogue as a revival of the Academic custom condemned by Augustine. In a novel and un-Ciceronian manner, he consciously exploits the discrepancy between speaker and viewpoint, both as a means of dealing with a controversial topic and as a mode of examining arguments without reference to the authority of individuals.

The revival of the Academic method of argument in *De avaritia,* which characterizes Poggio's later dialogues as well, clearly reflects the direct encounter between the humanist's ideal of discussion and the historical obstacle posed by Augustine. In striving to re-establish the Ciceronian model of structure and method for the dialogue, Poggio had to confront the Augustinian objections voiced in *Contra Academicos.* In so doing, Poggio has in part adopted the structure of *Contra Academicos,* in which an initial two-part debate is subsequently resolved by a religious figure with Christian authority. At the same time, Poggio has reduced the authority of Scripture to a secular level of judgment subject to rational examination, as one of the "voices of truth itself," and Augustine himself is cited by three of the interlocutors of *De avaritia* for various purposes. Antonio quotes Augustine's definition of avarice in order to defend the deadly sin which Augustine would have condemned (I, 12). Cincio cites Augustine's complaint against the avaricious clergy for his own polemical purposes (I, 22). Andreas quotes Augustine, who likens the avaricious to heretics (I, 29), but he characterizes this Augustinian comparison in classicizing terms, calling it a "divine saying issued from God's oracle" (*sententiam divinam tam ex oraculo Dei emissam*).

Like Petrarch before him, Poggio does not argue merely from authority and reason but appeals to experience as well, especially in Antonio's defense of avarice. This experience is not the personal experience of an individual, as in Petrarch, but the collective experience of contemporary practice. Poggio is the first to advance the criterion of usage later expounded by Valla and Pontano, for whom usage generally assumes a linguistic connotation. Valla and Pontano both assert that all philosophy must derive from correct linguistic usage, since language properly employed corresponds to the immediate reality of human experience. This linguistic approach to philosophy is already implicit in Poggio's *De avaritia*. In a significant passage, Antonio says that we must not regulate our lives by the standards of philosophy (I, 16: *vita mortalium non est exigenda nobis ad stateram philosophiae*). This assertion echoes Cicero's description of the orator's language in *De oratore* II, where Antonius observes that the orator deals with questions that are weighed "not in the goldsmith's balance, but in a sort of popular scale" (II, 38, 159: *non aurificis statera, sed populari quadam trutina*). Poggio thus anticipates the "rhetorical" philosophy of Valla, who quotes the Ciceronian passage in his *Dialecticae disputationes*.[18]

Following the methodological hints of Petrarch's *Secretum*, the prerequisite to the search for truth in Poggio's dialogues is the freedom, repeatedly asserted, of each person to form and maintain his own opinion. This freedom, which is essential to the spirit of dialogue, is a dominant theme in the dialogues of Cicero, and is revived by Petrarch in his *Secretum*.[19] In *De avaritia*, Antonio introduces the defense of avarice by professing to follow the custom of the ancient Academics, arguing the opposite position to that already heard and allowing the hearers to judge for themselves (I, 6). Introducing the discussion of fortune in his *De varietate fortunae*, Poggio says that he does not wish to oppose Aristotle and Aquinas; still, "since everyone is free to believe what he will," a discussion is possible (II, 529). At the conclusion of the dialogue *De nobilitate*, Niccoli leaves the final decision of the question of nobility to those with "a keener talent for debate; all are free to feel as they will" (I, 83). In his *Contra hypocritas* Poggio asserts the right of others to their own opinion before he expresses his own (II, 78); and in his *Historia convivialis* he begins the debate concerning medicine and law by expressing his own doubts on the subject, leaving the solution of the problem to his more perceptive companions (I, 37). Introducing the discussion in *De miseria humanae conditionis*, Cosimo de' Medici says that the validity of the arguments presented may be judged by those with greater learning; he himself will speak whatever comes to mind, while others may maintain their own opinions (I, 94).

The freedom of opinion established in the dialogues applies to Poggio's readers as well as to his interlocutors. Thus, in the preface to his *An seni sit uxor ducenda*, Poggio writes to Cosimo de' Medici that he is sending him the dialogue in order to elicit his opinion (II, 684). Similarly, in *De varietate fortunae*, Antonio Loschi exhorts anyone who is qualified for the task to narrate contemporary history, and he later asserts the right of readers to judge for themselves concerning historical writings (II, 537, 580)—such as, by implication, the dialogue itself.

The interaction of dialogue and reader is essential to Poggio's notion of progress in literary and philosophical endeavors. In the preface to *De avaritia* Poggio writes that he has published his dialogue as a small beginning from which others may produce a more perfect or elegant treatment of the subject: "It seemed to me enough to publish my little efforts (for what they are worth), from which those wishing to undertake the task of revision and fuller exposition might derive and perfect something more complete" (I,1).[20] His reasons for publishing *De nobilitate* are the same; and in his preface to that dialogue, Poggio expounds his conception of progress in philosophy, a notion derived from Cicero's *Brutus*:

> It seemed reasonable to me to publish a sort of beginning for the treatment of this topic, which more learned men, aroused by me, might afterwards render more polished and elegant with their wisdom. For in every endeavor, the first to write about a subject have generally been considered less brilliant and refined. Nothing has ever arisen at the outset both invented and established without later generations adding to it and improving it. Even in philosophy, the mother of wisdom, and in the liberal arts, we see that this has been the case: since all of them arrived at the peak of perfection by degrees, it was enough for the originators to provide some

> incitements and give the spur, as it were, to others for seeking greater perfection. In the same way, I expect that this essay of mine will arouse someone with talent to apply himself to improving whatever he sees I have omitted or mistaken. (I, 64)[21]

The related notion of challenge (*provocatio*), in the sense of both promoting debate within the dialogue and eliciting response from readers, is found in Poggio's preface to his *De infelicitate principum*: "When I found the time, I wrote down this discussion once held between learned men, so that whoever might wish to write more copiously on the subject may have greater ability as a result of my challenge" (I, 394).[22] In his preface to the second book of *De miseria humanae conditionis*, Poggio repeats the notion of progress in the arts and the hope that others may be aroused to improve upon his work:

> I ask my readers to consider this treatment written not as a display of my talent but as an exercise of my wits. I deemed it better to spend what little time might be free from my affairs in praiseworthy endeavors, rather than to waste it in lazy and sluggish idleness. Others perhaps will be aroused to treat this material more copiously and learnedly, thereby contributing much, in my opinion, to learned studies and to the sciences. For such great progress (*progressio*) would not have been made in philosophy or in any other excellent art if the earlier writers had not by their contributions offered matter for correction and profounder understanding. (I, 112)

Contrasted to the freedom of opinion among the learned friends in Poggio's dialogues is an awareness of the need for restraint in alluding specifically to contemporaries. In publishing his *De avaritia*, Poggio was afraid of offending contemporaries, notably Bruni.[23] Within the dialogue itself Bartolomeo expresses a reluctance to use examples which might offend (I, 4: *Nolo exemplis uti, ne quem mea verba offendant*). In the third book of his *De varietate fortunae* Poggio fears to offend contemporaries if he narrates recent history, citing the Terentian dictum that the truth breeds enmity (II, 591).[24] In his *De infelicitate principum* Poggio similarly chooses to abstain from discussing the happiness of popes (I, 397). Although in the same dialogue Poggio attributes freedom of expression to the Florentine Niccoli, even the latter soon explains that he is speaking not about specific individuals but about the subject in general (I, 397). Likewise, in *Contra hypocritas* Carlo Marsuppini cautions Poggio against discussing the pope in order to avoid giving offense; and after a pointed remark concerning the late Eugenius IV, Poggio consents to pass over pontifical examples (II, 75). A similar fear of recriminations from the clergy is expressed by Cosimo de' Medici in *De miseria humanae conditionis* (I, 100). After a general denunciation of mendicants in the same work, Matteo Palmieri proposes to leave them in their erroneous felicity lest he provoke them (I, 102). When Cosimo later asks about the happiness of popes, Poggio confesses his inability to speak freely on the subject (I, 115).

The fear of offending others thus constitutes the negative complement to Poggio's goal of arousing learned readers, by the positive *provocatio* of the dialogues, to participate in a continuing pursuit of truth and eloquence, as described in his theory of progress. On the one hand, Poggio strives to represent the freedom of opinion that promotes inquiry; on the other, he fears offending contemporaries who may resent his moral pronouncements. Yet Poggio's dialogues also contain a great deal of open polemic, generally aimed at the group which humanists condemned most and feared least, the friars of the mendicant orders.

In *De avaritia*, Cincio is the most outspoken critic of the clergy. During the initial discussion of Bernardino, Cincio attacks the vainglory of contemporary preachers, who seek the applause rather than the spiritual improvement of their hearers (I, 2-3). Later in the discussion, after Andreas has argued that not all men are moved by avarice, Cincio sarcastically comments that Antonio's general attribution of avarice is intended to refer only to priests, and he traces the avarice of priests to the greed of Judas, adding the testimonies of Augustine and Petrarch on clerical corruption. Yet even Cincio recognizes the need for silence in this matter, observing acidly that it is better to be silent about avaricious priests than to say too little (I, 22). Andreas resumes his discourse, noting that the purpose of their discussion does not properly admit this question.

In general, the anger of powerful individuals is what Poggio seeks to avoid, but his interlocutors also manifest caution in alluding to the masses. In *De miseria humanae conditionis*, Cosimo de' Medici deprecates allusions to his own family lest they arouse envy, adding that in order to avoid the unstable opinion of the mob, he will restrict his discussion to ancient examples: "Let us cease . . . to speak of ourselves, lest we seem to indulge in self-praise, which would cause envy. Yet I can truly observe that many of our citizens died happily, whose names I omit in order to avoid the unstable judgment of the masses; I may more properly confine my remarks to citing ancient examples" (I, 94). This dismissal of fluctuating popular opinion (*vulgi varia sentientis opinio*) is an important feature of Poggio's dialogues. Surprisingly, it is Antonio in *De avaritia* who insists "that we argue not according to popular judgment, but by reason" (I, 10), for much of his defense of avarice relies on the citing of example and usage. Otherwise, it is the Stoic idealist Niccoli who rejects unstable popular opinion in order to affirm the eternal truths discovered by reason. This antithesis is central to the argument of *De nobilitate*, as in Niccoli's reply to the concept of nobility derived by Lorenzo de' Medici from common usage:

> "Do you think," said Niccolò, "that we should argue by the judgment of learned men or by that of the masses and populace? For if you are swayed by the opinions and customs of men, you will see that there is no foundation for the concept of nobility: these are so various and contradictory that I fail to see what standard of nobility they offer. The word exists everywhere, but the thing differs . . . Now if there is such a thing as nobility and if it has a source (as we must admit) in a certain reality and reason, then it must be one and the same everywhere. Yet since the opinion of the masses values nothing less than virtue or reason . . . I often am forced to think that "nobility" is merely an empty name." (I, 66)

Similarly, in *De infelicitate principum* Niccoli asserts that the truth, not popular opinion, is the object of the inquiry (I, 395: *non existimationem vulgi, sed veritatem quaerimus*).

The humanist circle dipicted in Poggio's dialogues thus places itself in the position of an educated minority, elevated above the masses and above the clergy who exploit the masses. Like Cicero's dialogues, Poggio's dialogues depict a select gathering of learned company. Yet Ciceronian leisure (*otium*) suggests the occupations (*negotium*) of the interlocutors' daily affairs, whereas the settings of Poggio's dialogues both imply a respite from the turmoil of the Curia (which was subject to frequent disturbances in the first half of the Quattrocento) and create a sort of literary immunity for the discussion of controversial topics. Poggio's dialogues are characterized by an innovative and polemical treatment of contemporary questions of morality, and thus their setting reflects the caution necessary in expounding controversial views.[25] The provocative intent of the dialogues extends especially to Poggio's readership, and by the composition of his last dialogue, *De miseria humanae conditinis* (1455), Poggio's faith lies rather in the formative value of writing than in an enthusiasm for personal debate.[26] Yet as a vivid record of the humanists' discussions during the early Quattrocento and of their novel concerns and attitudes, Poggio's dialogues are unequaled.

IV

Lorenzo Valla and the Rhetorical Dialogue

Although the philosophers call themselves the guides of all others even in our day, yet the reality shows that it is the orators who should be called the guides and leaders of the others.

THE PRINCIPAL LATIN dialogues of Lorenzo Valla (1405-1457)—his *De vero falsoque bono* (1431-1441), *De libero arbitrio* (1439), and *De professione religiosorum* (1442)—portray the lively confrontation of the new critical spirit of humanism with traditional moral and religious problems. In the last two dialogues, the discussion is confined to two interlocutors, and it is easy to identify the Socratic method of "Laurentius" with the author's own acute reasonings. *De vero falsoque bono,* on the contrary, has been the object of various interpretations because of its provocative and ambiguous nature.[1] As an example of the form of dialogue employed by the first generation of Quattrocento humanists, Valla's *De vero falsoque bono* both continues the tradition of Bruni's *Dialogi ad Petrum Histrum* and Poggio's *De avaritia* and represents the culmination of the early humanist dialogue.

Although Valla revised his first dialogue several times, its structure remained substantially the same from the earliest version, *De voluptate,* published in Piacenza in 1431, to the final version, *De vero falsoque bono,* elaborated in Naples after 1441 (pp. xxx-lvii). Comprising three books, *De vero falsoque bono* portrays a discussion of the highest ethical good. It is set in Pavia and consists principally of three lengthy discourses expounding Stoic, Epicurean, and Christian doctrines. In the first book, the jurist Catone Sacco, identified as a

Stoic, voices a complaint against man's natural condition; he is answered by the poet Maffeo Vegio, who delivers an Epicurean encomium of man's earthly pleasures. In the second book, Vegio refutes the notion of Stoic virtue (*honestas*), exploding its traditional categories and exemplars. In the third book, a verdict on the first two speakers is pronounced by the theologian Antonio da Rho, who judges their classicizing arguments from a Christian point of view and concludes with an elaborate panegyric of celestial pleasures. An epilogue to the discussion is provided by the educator Guarino of Verona, who judges the eloquence of Vegio and Antonio, whereupon the gathering ends.

The title and argument of Valla's *De vero falsoque bono* recall Cicero's dialogue *De finibus bonorum et malorum*. Where Cicero's work expounds and evaluates the highest ethical good as successively defined by Epicurean, Stoic, and Peripatetic interlocutors, Valla's dialogue presents interlocutors who advance Stoic, Epicurean, and Christian interpretations of the topic. Yet the resemblance is misleading, for *De finibus* examines the three ancient schools in separate discussions, whereas *De vero falsoque bono* assembles the proponents of various doctrines in a single gathering which seeks a synthetic judgment. In this respect, Valla's dialogue bears a greater resemblance to Cicero's *De natura deorum*, in which the author's own position—like that of Valla—remains ambiguous.[2]

Following the example of Poggio, Valla has modified his Ciceronian model along Augustinian lines, and the influence of Augustine's Cassiciacum dialogues is evident in his organization of the argument. As Poggio's *De avaritia* imitates Augustine's dialogues by presenting a two-part debate judged by the Christian theologian Andreas of Constantinople, so Valla's *De vero falsoque bono* depicts a debate between two classical philosophies, adjudicated by the Christian theologian Antonio da Rho. The resemblance of Valla's Antonio to the Augustine of *Contra Academicos* is striking. In the first book of *Contra Academicos*, Augustine says that he has permitted Licentius and Trygetius to debate because he wishes them to exercise themselves (I, 9, 24: *PL*, 32, 918). Similarly, Antonio in the third book of Valla's *De vero falsoque bono* hopes that Catone and Maffeo have disputed in the manner of the ancients only for the sake of the exercise (p. 106). Both Augustine and Antonio welcome the classical arguments which facilitate their task of expounding the Christian truth. In the second book of *Contra Academicos*, Augustine rejoices that his friend Alypius has espoused Academic views which will, by contrast, illuminate his Christian doctrine (II, 13, 20: *PL*, 32, 934). Likewise, Valla's

Antonio says that he has allowed Catone and Maffeo to play the roles of Stoic and Epicurean because their debate reveals their common error (p. 106).

Another Augustinian source has determined Valla's reworking of the Ciceronian form of the dialogue. The opposition of Stoic and Epicurean doctrines to a spiritual notion of the highest good derives from Augustine's Epistle 118 to Dioscorus, written in 410, in which Augustine, as bishop of Hippo, comments on Cicero's philosophical works in response to Dioscorus' inquiry. In his epistle, Augustine discusses the *summum bonum*, or highest good, of three philosophcal sects, the Stoics, Epicureans, and Neoplatonists. Implicitly identifying the Neoplatonic ideal with the Christian notion of a celestial good, Augustine suggests the basic constitution of Valla's debate in an image of warring sects. The Neoplatonists, he writes, saw fit to oppose the Stoics and Epicureans above all others in defining the highest good:

> Concerning the question of man's highest good, remove the specific persons and set up the debate by itself. You will find that two erroneous positions clash against one another in direct opposition, one placing the highest good in the body, and the other in the mind. The reason of truth, by which we know that God is our highest good, is opposed to both of them, first unteaching their base principles and then teaching the true ones. Now arrange the debate by adding the persons. You will find the Epicureans and Stoics battling fiercely between themselves, while the Neoplatonists attempt to adjudicate their difference, concealing their own opinion of the truth while convicting and refuting the others' vain faith in falsehood. (*PL*, 33, 440)

This passage from Augustine clearly suggests the image of Stoic and Epicurean philosophers in battle, which Valla also envisions in his proem to Book I: "If Jesus Himself gives me the shield of faith and the sword of the spirit as I enter this battle to fight for His honor, how can we not expect to win the victory? Just as David used his enemy's own sword to kill him, and as Jonathan forced his adversaries to turn their swords against themselves, so I hope in part to slay these gentiles, the philosophers, and in part to rouse them to an internecine war and their self-destruction, by the power of our faith, such as it is, and of God's word" (p. 2).[3] More important, Augustine's epistle formulates the duality of celestial truth and terrestrial falsehood underlying the argument of Valla's *De vero falsoque bono*, in which the false good of ancient philosophy is refuted in order to expound the truth of the Christian faith. Indeed, declaring this purpose in his proem to Book I, Valla professes to follow the example of the Church Fathers Lactantius and Augustine, "the first of whom, coming earlier, seems to have confuted the false religions most admirably, as the second confirmed the true one" (p. 1).[4]

In Epistle 118 Augustine also notes the pre-eminence of the Stoics and Epicureans among classical sects, adducing as evidence of their importance the allusion to them in Acts of the Apostles 17:18. The same scriptural passage is cited in Valla's dialogue, when Antonio intercedes in Book III—as Augustine had in his *Contra Academicos*—to commend the previous disputants on their classical learning and to adjudicate their debate:

> Let us now return to judging your disagreement and to demonstrating the highest good. One of you places the only, or highest, good in virtue; the other in pleasure, each one defending his own of these two opposed philosophical sects. This happened quite opportunely, and I have thus willingly allowed you to speak like representatives of the ancient philosophers, since in this way your common error will the more readily appear. Your dispute was all the more enjoyable because you argued as if intentionally about the two sects which are to my mind the noblest. My view is confirmed by many proofs, including the passage in the Acts of the Apostles [17:18] where only the Epicureans and the Stoics are mentioned, whom we see to have flourished at that time more than the others in Athens, the very seat of learning and the cradle of philosophy. (p. 101)[5]

Like Poggio, Valla constitutes his dialogue by mixing Ciceronian and Augustinian elements; but Valla's debt to Augustine is even more profound and complex than Poggio's. Augustine's Epistle 118 had warned that some classical philosophers, notable the Stoics, had placed the highest good in the mind, not in the body, but that their doctrine still failed to attain the higher Christian truth (*PL*, 33, 439-440). Valla in turn exploits this notion of Stoicism as a dangerously attractive falsehood and places the Stoic speaker first in order to refute him the more thoroughly: "Since it is the Stoics who most violently assert virtue, I have seen fit to regard them as our adversaries . . . While all three books serve to refute and demolish this Stoic breed, the first proves pleasure the only good, the second proves the philosophers' virtue not a good at all, and the third treats of the true and the false good. The last book will appropriately provide a sort of lucid panegyric to summon the souls of our readers to hope for the true good" (pp. 2-3). Cicero had placed Epicurean doctrines first as the easiest to understand (*De fin.*, I, 5, 13); Valla expounds Stoic doctrines first and gives the central and dominant role to the Epicurean. Although the refutation of the Stoics is in accordance with Augustine's warning against them, Valla's method of espousing Epicureanism to refute Stoicism runs directly counter to the notion of Augustine, who conceived of the search for truth and God as an ascent from the corporeal to the spiritual (*Conf.*, VII, 17, 23). Valla, on the contrary, denies the Stoic abstractions in favor of the corporeal realities of the Epicureans, in an ostensible descent to concrete ethical values.

Valla's dialogue continues the provocative method of argumentation established by the dialogues of Bruni and Poggio, with which Valla's work is connected by historical circumstances and by internal structural features. Valla conceived his first dialogue while employed in the Roman Curia, where he had met both Bruni and Poggio. Poggio's dialogue *De avaritia* was published in 1430. Valla published his dialogue after leaving the Curia in the following year, giving it the provocative title *De voluptate* as if to link it with Poggio's work, which had clearly influenced him. Set in the Roman Curia, the original version of Valla's dialogue depicts both Poggio and Valla as present in the discussion, while the selection of Bruni and Niccoli as two of the principal interlocutors suggests the influence of Bruni's *Dialogi*.

On a smaller scale, Bruni's *Dialogi ad Petrum Histrum* foreshadow the structure of Valla's *De vero falsoque bono*, and certain literary devices used by Bruni reappear in Valla's dialogue. In *Dialogus I*, which corresponds to Valla's Books I and II, Niccoli actuates the debate by condemning the unfavorable conditions of the age, which make literary studies impossible. Book I of *De vero falsoque bono* begins similarly with Catone's denunciation of nature's malignity, which impedes man's moral perfection. In Bruni, Niccoli's charges are answered by Salutati's praise of Dante, Petrarch, and Boccaccio; in Valla, Catone's tirade is rebutted by Vegio's encomium of nature, which ends Book I. Bruni's Niccoli impugns the value of the Florentine poets in an attack which concludes *Dialogus I*; in Valla's Book II, Vegio proceeds to a systematic denunciation of Stoic virtues.

In each work, the authors are described as initially agreeing with the controversial speaker—Bruni with Niccoli and Valla with Vegio—but as finally joining the consensus established in the conclusion.[6] Adopting a broader historical and political view of Florentine culture, the Niccoli of Bruni's *Dialogus II* recants his previous position and lauds the Florentine poets, while the Antonio of Valla's Book III (Niccoli in *De voluptate*), embracing the universal context of Christian salvation, rejects ancient philosophy and pronounces a panegyric on celestial beatitude. In each dialogue, the last book is set in a garden, the movement to which symbolizes the shifting of the discussion to a higher plane of understanding and agreement.[7] Bruni's device for cutting short the discussion of *Dialogus I*—the setting of the sun causes Salutati to postpone his defense of the Florentine poets (p. 74)—is adopted by Valla in Book III of *De vero falsoque bono*, when the setting sun forces Antonio to be brief, thereby allowing him to avoid discussion of the medieval topic of infernal torments (p.117).

The affinities of Valla's *De vero falsoque bono* with Poggio's *De avaritia* are even more striking, and there is no doubt that Valla learned much from Poggio's dialogue. Each work features three principal interlocutors who participate in a discussion modeled on that of Augustine's *Contra Academicos*, and the initial classicizing debate of each is finally judged by a revered Christian authority, in both cases a theologian. Yet both dialogues also engage in an implicit polemic with Augustine, and the provocative second speaker is not merely a devil's advocate to be confuted in the conclusion. Rather, both Poggio's Loschi and Valla's Vegio establish a radical method of argumentation which runs counter to Augustine's strictures on Academic debate, and both argue from everyday realities for self-interest (*utilitas*) as the universal motivation in ethical doctrine.[8]

Both Poggio and Valla revised their dialogues, and their revisions in selecting interlocutors indicate a common notion of dialogue. In both cases there is evidence that the structure of the dialogue was independent of the choice of interlocutors: Poggio's revisions on Niccoli's advice and Valla's substitution of both principal and secondary speakers from the *De voluptate* to the *De vero falsoque bono* demonstrate the flexibility of the dialogue framework. Yet even in the choice of interlocutors similarities are apparent. Both Poggio and Valla chose unlikely exponents for the first two positions argued in their dialogues but strove for verisimilitude in the choice of the final speaker. For his first speaker, who attacks avarice, Poggio at first had selected Cincio, known to be avaricious; at Loschi's insistence he substituted Bartolomeo. Similarly, Valla's selection of Catone Sacco to deliver Stoic and Aristotelian remarks seems contradictory to the views of the historical Sacco; Bruni, Valla's first choice, was perhaps more suitable (pp. xxiv-xlvii, 107).

In both Poggio and Valla, the second speaker is a sort of *advocatus diaboli*, and both writers chose interlocutors easily exonerated from charges of espousing sincerely the positions which are attributed to them in the dialogues. As his defender of avarice, Poggio chose the liberal Loschi and called attention to the contradiction in the dialogue itself, as well as in his letters to Niccoli. As his provocative Epicurean, Valla first selected Panormita, probably for the poetic license necessary in the dialogue. The ironies inherent in the defense of worldly pleasure were subsequently heightened by Valla's substitution of Vegio for Panormita; as in Poggio, the ethical contradiction involved is noted by the interlocutors (p. 107). For the third speaker, who in each work provides a Christian resolution of the problems, both Poggio and Valla selected men known for their learning and piety. To be sure, Valla's original choice, Niccoli, seems problematic in the light of his modern reputation as a contentious and difficult scholar, but there is no reason to see an ironic intention in Valla's first selection.[9] Poggio intentionally chose Andreas of Constantinople for his piety and for the suitability of his religious quotations. The same criteria are evident in Valla's selection of Antonio as the final speaker in *De vero falsoque bono* (pp. xlvii, 93-94).

Poggio's *De avaritia* and Valla's *De vero falsoque bono* share a similar organization of arguments. Poggio's dialogue begins its discussion of avarice with Bartolomeo's attack on the vice, and Valla's work grows out of the problems posed by Catone's accusation of nature. These opening speeches are answered by Loschi's defense of avarice and by Vegio's defense of nature. The final speaker in both Poggio and Valla responds to the previous interlocutors, first along the classicizing lines established by them, and then in the light of scriptural authority and Christian revelation. In each case, the critique of the classical thesis is twofold but acknowledges the validity of a thesis which the second speaker proposed. Thus, Andreas in *De avaritia* rejects the definition of avarice offered by Loschi and denies that avarice is natural; at the same time, he accepts the existence of a natural impulse which he calls *cupiditas* (I, 18). In Book III of *De vero falsoque bono,* Antonio systematically refutes both theses which Catone had advanced in Book I—the Aristotelian scheme of virtue and man's natural impulse toward vice—but allows the validity of Vegio's preference of *voluptas* over *honestas* (p. 110). These verdicts in classical terms are followed in both dialogues by Christian homilies on the eternal truth revealed in Scripture: both Poggio's Andreas and Valla's Antonio conclude with elevated discourses in which Pauline and patristic texts supplant the previous classical allusions.[10] The end of each dialogue presents the humanist circle's approbation of the third speaker. In Poggio, the discussion ends with citations from Lucian, Silius Italicus, and Cicero, as well as with the capitulation of Loschi; in Valla, the peroration of Antonio is followed by Guarino's pronouncement on Maffeo's and Antonio's eloquence, after which the gathering is dissolved.

Unlike Cicero's *De finibus,* Valla's *De vero falsoque bono* does not consistently ascribe philosophical positions to interlocutors known for holding such views. Rather, like Poggio's *De avaritia,*

Valla's dialogue establishes an initial debate in which the rhetorical aspect is heightened by implicit contradictions between speaker and speech. Such contradictions are not merely implicit. In Poggio, when the final speaker assumes his role of refuting the previous speakers, he excuses their unorthodox statements and insists on the artificial and insincere nature of their remarks. The attitude of Augustine toward his pupils Licentius and Trygetius in *Contra Academicos* is recalled when Antonio expresses his hope that Catone and Maffeo have maintained their positions in imitation of ancient debates: "God forbid that you wanted to affirm the Stoic doctrine, Catone, and you the Epicurean, Vegio, rather than to display your pleasure in reproducing ancient matters and customs in a discussion undertaken for the sake of exercise or for its novelty." Antonio notes the discrepancy between Vegio's piety and his words, attributing it to Vegio's playful emulation of Socratic irony:

> Which of us, Vegio, has any doubts about you? Your speech was more suited to corrupting our minds . . . but you were unlike yourself since you usually not only live but even speak in a different manner . . . I know you well enough to realize that you don't mean what you say. As a result, I suspect that you spoke not in earnest but in jest, as you often do, in the fashion of the ironic Socrates . . . You spoke feignedly, which you would not have done (at least not rightly) with a different audience. But you had no need to fear corrupting such worthy men with your speech, and it was only natural to reply that way to Catone, who had begun in the manner of the ancients. (p. 106)

Catone, in contrast, had spoken seriously in Antonio's opinion, but only because his enthusiasm for classical philosophy made him forget the truths of Christianity:

> Catone, whose speech seems nearer the truth, undoubtedly spoke in earnest and did not begin the discussion as a jest. What then? Shall we say he was wrong? No, for Catone is not given to error, but he wanted to show himself an admirer of antiquity. Now, I grant the ancients their literature, their studies, and (most valuable of all) their oratory, but I deny that they achieved wisdom and a knowledge of true virtue. Yet I don't wish to address you, Catone, as if you were a defender of the Stoics, for I know you are a pious advocate of the faith as well as of lawsuits, and I have heard you often remark that you have perused all the books on our religion which merit reading, so that you can compare them and explain what is best in each. Why then should I contradict you, who agree with me, although you spoke otherwise? (p. 107)

Valla's *De vero falsoque bono* is a rhetorical dialogue in two senses. First, it depicts an oratorical debate conceived as a sort of forensic case argued before a bench of humanist judges. Second, the declared method of argumentation is rhetorical as opposed to dialectical: rhetoric is in fact asserted as superior to philosophy throughout the work. In part, Valla's methodology derives from Cicero's declaration of the orator's eclectic freedom; and to that extent Valla's dialogue continues the revival of Academic skepticism begun in Poggio's dialogues.

As refuters of the abstract dogmatism of their Stoic opponents, both Vegio and Antonio assert the orator's Ciceronian freedom to argue without tendentious allegiance to a single philosophical sect. At the beginning of his reply to Catone, Vegio advances the methodological thesis of the dialogue, the superiority of rhetoric to philosophy: "anyone may seek support for his cause from whatever source he pleases . . . This is especially true for me, since I have been initiated not in the rites of philosophy, but in the greater and more excellent rites of rhetoric and poetry. For philosophy is a sort of soldier or tribune under the command of oratory, which a great tragedian calls a queen. And Cicero rightly allowed himself the freedom of discussing what he chose in philosophy without allegiance to a single sect."[12] As Hanna-Barbara Gerl has shown, Valla's preference for rhetoric over philosophy is part of a serious and coherent program to replace abstract logic with inductive rhetoric.[13] In the critical spirit of Valla's thorough scrutiny of Western thought, Vegio laments even Cicero's occasional inconsistency: "I only wish he had not said that he would treat the subject as a philosopher, but as an orator, and had exercised even more this license, or liberty rather, by demanding back from the philosophers whatever rhetorical apparatus he found in them (for all things claimed by the philosophers are ours), and if they had resisted, had wielded the sword given him by Queen Eloquence in the philosophers' lairs, putting them to death" (p. 14).[14]

In the same fashion, Antonio in Book III demonstrates the superiority of Cicero to Boethius in perceiving the ambiguity of the term *bonum*. The example leads to a comparison of oratory's abundant resources with the limited strength of dialectic:

> While both beatitude and virtue are called "good," the "good" are those possessed of virtue, not of happiness and beatitude. In this Boethius was deceived, being fonder of the dialecticians than of the rhetoricians. But how much better it would have been to speak rhetorically than

> dialectically! What could be more absurd than to risk the whole cause on one word, as the philosophers do? An orator, on the contrary, uses many varied arguments, cites the opposite cases, adduces examples, compares similes, and forces even the hidden truth to emerge. How wretched and poor is a commander who risks the entire outcome of the war on the life of one soldier! We must fight all together, and if one soldier falls or one tower is taken, we must replace them on the spot with new reinforcements. (p. 113)

Antonio's description of the rhetorical method—the varied arguments, examples, comparisons, and contrasts employed by the orator—aptly describes the method of the interlocutors in Valla's dialogue, which presents its discussion as a sort of humanist trial of ethical doctrines. The forensic nature of *De vero falsoque bono* as an orator's contest reveals the pervasive influence of Quintilian's *Institutio oratoria*, the most complete ancient Latin treatise on the orator and one of Valla's favorite books.

The initial exchange between Catone and Maffeo in Book I, their accusation and defense of nature, assumes the form of a trial, in which a courtroom atmosphere is established at the outset by the Stoic plaintiff Catone. When asked to speak on the subject of the highest ethical good, Catone praises his auditors and disclaims any ability to instruct them; even his attitude suggests a courtroom speech: "Then Catone, first fixing his eyes for a moment on the ground and then looking up at his hearers, began: 'I always find it more pleasant to listen to learned men than to speak to them, knowing that I can learn more than I can teach, and since you are doubtless the most prominent men of learning in our age, I have sought to confer with you. But since you, most prudent men, have decided that I should speak first of all, I shall perform your bidding' " (p. 4).

Catone proceeds to a twofold accusation of nature, alleging that vices outnumber virtues and that man is born with a propensity to vice rather than virtue. Each point is argued with the kinds of proof that Antonio will later ascribe to the orator: he adduces examples and compares analogies (p. 113: *exempla repetit, similitudines comparat*). Catone's first charge, concerning the difficulty of attaining the virtuous mean between vicious excesses, is principally supported by historical examples, namely Crassus, Cato, and Catiline; his second charge, concerning man's innate proclivity to vice, relies more on literary examples and quotations, from Ovid, Horace, Virgil, and various myths (pp. 4-11). This preponderance of historical and poetic *exempla* is balanced by Vegio's defense of Epicurean pleasure in Book

I, which derives most of its arguments from poetic examples (pp. 36-42), and by Vegio's refutation of Stoic virtue in Book II, which treats the motives of celebrated historical figures (pp. 44-68).

The influence of Quintilian becomes evident as Catone ends his accusation of nature and addresses the defendant in impassioned accents:

> If Nature herself could come forth and appear before us, I dare say (and you may believe me) I would exact the reason for her acts and address her thus: "In such a manner are you pleased to treat us, Nature, whom we believe and call our mother, that you provide us with such scant forces against so great a host, that for this difficult conflict you have given us a mind which prefers defeat to victory, and that unless we win a clear victory, you persecute us with an immediate and terrible vengeance? Do you hope to compel us with blows, like children? You must proceed another way! That, O harsh one, is not approved even for children . . . A suppliant I stretch forth my hands, and falling at your feet, I clutch you. If you are our mother, as you certainly must be, grant that we your children may recognize you once more. Imagine all the peoples, even those you think haughty and hostile, imagine them lying squalid and deformed (*squalidos, deformes*), consumed with groans and tears." (p. 11)[15]

Catone's peroration combines the classical prosopopoeia (*ficta oratio*) of his address to nature with the plea for pity (*miseratio*) of introducing his clients (all mankind, the children of nature) as "squalid and deformed," which Quintilian prescribes.[16]

In order to dispel the serious impression made by Catone's speech, Vegio replies to him in a tone of mild amusement: "Although it is a great and worthy topic we discuss, and I see Catone moved in both his words and his mind, yet I can't keep from laughing" (p. 12). Vegio makes an ethical comparison of his adversary and himself:

> We read that whenever a certain Heraclius went out and saw men's deeds, he used to bewail men as madmen, while Democritus was only seen in public laughing: what one wept over, the other laughed at. I should compare you to Heraclius since you weep for men, although you don't weep so often, fearing no doubt to weep your eyes out, for Juvenal wonders that this didn't happen to Heraclius. But although I have laughed long, you can't compare me to Democritus, for I do not laugh at all men, but only at one man who bewails his fellows. And if you think me like Democritus, he of course used to laugh at Heraclius; for the latter was a Stoic before the Stoics, and Democritus the teacher of Epicurus. (pp. 12-13)

Vegio continues, as Catone had begun, modestly addressing his auditors in order to win their favor and approval: "I have not undertaken the task of replying, most excellent men, rashly or presumptuously. As you are kindly disposed toward me, you will forgive my desire to speak as an Epicurean against this Stoic." On behalf of the group, Giuseppe Bripi welcomes Vegio's defense of nature (p. 13: *patrocinium naturae*).

After further expressions of humility, Vegio begins his critique of Stoicism according to rhetorical criteria, attacking the Stoics for their obscure expression and rigid pessimism. He is careful to except Catone from both stylistic and ethical charges. Praising oratory as superior to philosophy, Vegio evokes the image of squalid philosophers and their obscure disputes: "How much more clear, grave, and magnificent were the orators in discussing the subject than the obscure, squalid, and lifeless philosophers in debating it! I have said this to indicate my wish that we discuss this source of philosophical contention in our rhetorical fashion, as I see Catone has wisely done" (p. 15).[17] He caricatures the Stoic philosophers as gloomy and stubborn (*tristes quidam et rigidi*) and as invidiously defaming mankind. Vegio argues for the benevolence of nature and ends the exordium with a statement of the real difference between his position and Catone's: "The great question between us lies in what should be called good. Let us examine and evaluate these two views: if we should refer everything to pleasure and nothing to virtue, then I maintain that neither of your premises is valid" (p. 20).

Catone objects to Vegio's investigation of this problem on the grounds that such a dispute cannot be treated fancifully: "Arguing with you is not like arguing with an opponent. I see that you are determined to speak poetically, that is, to embellish the falsehoods of your position with sugared phrases." Echoing Quintilian, Vegio counters by impugning the stubbornness of the Stoics; he himself views the debate as a court case argued to elicit the truth:

> Above all I wish to ask that we not proceed with that troublesome obstinacy of the Stoics. They think it unlawful to abandon a belief once they have adopted it (*nefas esse a suscepta semel persuasione discedere*), and never surrender, preferring to be slaughtered rather than conquered in a debate, like raging beasts or tigers that cannot be taken alive. As for me, if someone makes a better point than I do, I yield, and am grateful besides. For the business of forensics is not for one advocate to defeat another in a case, but to reveal either the truth or justice by their struggle. I should not call an orator anyone who denies this obvious fact. (p. 20)[18]

Vegio elaborates his concept of the orator, adding to his previous praise moral and philosophical considerations derived from Quintilian: "Even the most eloquent orator is a true orator only if he is good, for there is nothing more pernicious than a wicked man of learning. I would not bother to tell you this, Catone, if I thought you simply an orator, not obliged to swear to observe the laws of any one sect (*in cuiuspiam secte iurare leges*). But as I see you now so attached to the Stoics' dogma, I fear somewhat lest you may violently resist the truth" (p. 20).[19] Vegio's insistence on the orator's freedom in philosophy echoes Book XII of *Institutio oratoria,* in which Quintilian discusses the contribution of various philosophical schools to the prospective orator's art:

> While the Stoics must admit that their teachers generally have lacked the fullness and brilliance of eloquence, they claim that no one argues as sharply or deduces more subtly than they do. But this they perform among themselves, and as if bound by sacred oath or even fettered by superstition, they think it unlawful to abandon a belief once they have adopted it (*nefas esse a suscepta semel persuasione discedere*). An orator, on the other hand, need not swear to observe anyone's laws (*in cuiusquam iurare leges*). (2, 25-26)

The twelfth book of Quintilian's *Institutio oratoria* is fundamental to the interpretation of both Vegio's defense of pleasure and Valla's concept of the dialogue, for it treats the problem of morality involved in arguing both sides of a question (the Ciceronian *in utramque partem disserere*). Valla insists that his own view is expressed in Antonio's Christian discourse in Book III, which notes the contradiction between Vegio's Epicurean speech and his Christian piety. Yet the largest part of *De vero falsoque bono* is attributed to Vegio, and the central role assigned to his "insincere" defense of pleasure requires explanation.

The beginning and end of Vegio's discourse provide the key to Valla's concept of the dialogue. At the outset of his discourse, Vegio echoes Quintilian's opinion, asserting that "even the most eloquent orator is a true orator only if he is good, for there is nothing more pernicious than a wicked man of learning" (p. 20). The pernicious aspect of eloquence in the service of evil is treated by Quintilian in a seminal passage, which suggests the image of nature as stepmother (*noverca*) in Catone's initial accusation:

> The orator whom I seek to define shall then be the same defined by Marcus Cato, "a good man skilled in speaking." Indeed, he shall above all be what

> Cato states first and what is most important by nature, a good man . . . For there is nothing more pernicious to public and private affairs than eloquence serving wickedness, and I myself, who have striven to contribute what I can to oratory, shall have done mankind a bad turn if I provide weapons to a robber rather than to a soldier. Yet why speak of myself? Nature herself will seem to have been not a mother, but a stepmother, in granting man a talent which separates him from other animals, if she devised the power of speech as an aid to crime, a foe to innocence, and an enemy of the truth . . . I do not simply assert that an orator should be a good man, but deny that anyone who is not a good man can become an orator.[20]

At the end of his exposition of Epicurean pleasure, Vegio alludes to the disquisitions of Carneades both for and against justice:

> Close to sharing my opinion was the famed Academic Carneades, who, fearing neither the Stoics nor the Peripatetics, safely argued both for and against justice, that is, spoke on both sides—for the useful and for the virtuous. This he did because he was obliged by the Academic rule not to reveal his own opinion, but to speak in favor of each side and against each side. But if like others he could have declared which was truer, I am sure he would have approved the side of advantage (*utilitas*); for his mind was incensed against the Stoics, whom he attacked hostilely. (p. 89)[21]

Vegio's conjecture that Carneades would have espoused Epicurean utility rather than Stoic virtue is one of the numerous instances of provocative irony which enliven the dialogue. The reference to Carneades at the end of Vegio's discourse, together with his opening remarks on the purpose of argument, suggest Quintilian's discussion in Book XII of *Institutio oratoria* about Carneades and the morality of arguing both sides of a question, which was the Academic method condemned by Augustine:[22]

> To consider how to speak in favor of falsehoods or even of injustices is not without use, if only because we may the more readily detect and refute them, just as one who knows what things are harmful will better apply a remedy. When the Academics speak on both sides of an argument, they do not necessarily live according to the lesser cause, and Carneades was not an unjust man although he is said to have spoken in the presence of Cato the Censor at Rome with equal force against justice, which he had defended the day before. Indeed, the nature of a virtue may be revealed by the vice, and equity becomes more apparent from a consideration of inequity; many things are proved by their opposites. An orator should know the devices of his opponents as a commander those of his enemy. (1, 34-36)

This passage contains the justification for Vegio's defense of pleasure, and it is not surprising to find in Quintilian the similes of medicine and warfare which are also employed by Valla—arguments as remedies (p. 1), the orator as military commander (pp. 2, 43).[23]

When Vegio begins his defense of nature and his refutation of the Stoics, Valla declares his support of the Epicurean position, adding "although we fear your proving your case, yet we hope that you will prove what you should desire most to prove" (p. 22). Valla's qualification of his support of Vegio is reflected in the ironies of Vegio's discourse. On the one hand, Vegio's Epicurean thesis establishes an important methodology, both by substituting concrete experience for *a priori* categories as the basis of ethical discussion and by asserting the superiority of rhetorical freedom over philosophical dogmatism—the principles that Valla wished Vegio to establish. On the other hand, Vegio's jocular tone and hyperbolic assertions cannot be taken seriously, even if they are consistent in an exaggerated manner with the psychology of the Epicurean position. While Vegio's positive contributions are subsequently adopted by Antonio in Book III, his unacceptable arguments are excused as ironic (p. 106).

Valla indicates the ambiguous nature of Vegio's discourse—useful methodologically, but inadequate ethically—by alluding to Quintilian's justification of Carneades. Accordingly, Vegio's Carneadean discourse is framed by observations which suggest the moral justification for arguing the objectionable side of a question as formulated in Quintilian's twelfth book: the orator's search for truth explores all possible arguments, and the adoption of an objectionable position may illuminate the validity of an acceptable one. Thus Vegio's praise of bodily pleasures establishes principles basic to Antonio's panegyric on spiritual joys. This sense of Vegio's defense is confirmed by Valla in the introduction to Book III of *De vero falsoque bono*, which begins with a paraphrase of Quintilian's proem to his twelfth book: "'We have come to the gravest part of my projected work,' as Quintilian says, 'and the sea bears our ships, as it were, until we no longer sight land, but only sea everywhere and the heavens' " (p. 91). For Quintilian, the most weighty part of his work is his treatment of the orator's moral qualities, a topic that not even Cicero had discussed (*Inst. orat.*, XII, pr. 2-4). For Valla, the most weighty part of his dialogue is the exposition of the Christian highest good, a doctrine which requires profound intellectual and moral qualities in its exponent.

In discussing the ethical prerequisites of the orator, both Quintilian and Valla cite the example of Demosthenes, who was reputed to be a bad man, but both attribute this reputation to the slanders of his enemies.[24] Both assert the necessity of moral integrity in the successful orator. Valla lists as the three qualities required of an exponent of divine matters "knowledge of divinity, integrity of life, and gravity of morals" (p. 91), thereby anticipating his description of Antonio as a man venerable for his great learning, his singular gravity, and his religious profession (p. 93). Valla places special emphasis on the notion of *gravitas*, both as a moral quality and as a stylistic trait. Thus, the shift from Vegio's feigned defense of pleasure to Antonio's devout teaching of salvation is marked by a shift from the humorous license of the former to the weighty dignity of the latter; and Quintilian's "gravest part"—invoked by Valla at the beginning of Book III—becomes, literally, the weightiest part of the dialogue in Antonio's grave discourse. It is an essential feature of Valla's rhetorical dialogue that matter, style, and personality correspond: knowledge, especially moral teaching, is inseparable from both psychology and expression.

The difference between Vegio's discourse and that of Antonio is structural as well as stylistic. To be sure, Vegio speaks before the others as an advocate before judges (p. 20), while Antonio in turn is asked to pronounce his judgment (pp. 93-94). Yet they both reply to Catone's accusation of nature, expound their own notions of the highest good, and conclude with elaborate perorations. The difference lies rather in the order of their remarks. Vegio begins his long discourse by stating the order of his defense: "I shall begin by confirming my cause, and then shall proceed to refuting the other" (p. 22). Since he is responding to Catone's accusation, his adopted order reverses the traditional method recommended by Quintilian: "if we plead first, we must begin by establishing our case and then proceed to refuting the arguments of the opposing side; if we reply, we should begin first with our refutation" (*Inst. orat.*, V, 13, 53). This reversal of the expected order undercuts the strength of Vegio's discourse; less emphasis is placed on the exposition of Epicurean pleasure in Book I than on the refutation of Stoic virtue in Book II. The discourse of Antonio in Book III, on the contrary, follows the prescribed rhetorical order by first refuting the positions of Catone and Vegio and then expounding the Christian doctrine which supersedes the classical notions of the highest good. Antonio emphasizes the Carneadean aspect of Vegio's discourse, which had subverted the classical cardinal virtues by deriving them from hedonistic motives, and challenges Vegio's sincerity, addressing himself at greater length to Catone's accusation of nature.

Antonio's discourse nevertheless adheres closely to the pattern established by the previous speakers. He disclaims any ability to instruct his auditors: "I am aware, most wise men, of your reasons for asking me to speak, although I am the least suitable person to choose in this matter, as you could gather from my silence today while I listened to these two. And if I were the right man to choose (which is not the case), you would not have chosen me in order to hear my opinion, for you are not so feeble-minded to ask me, as if more learned, to teach you what you could teach me" (p. 94). He answers the twofold accusation of Catone, relying more on rational argument than on poetic or historical example but remaining within the classical framework established by Catone. Having thus refuted on their own terms the classical doctrine of virtue and vice, Antonio introduces his judgment of Catone and Vegio by observing that the Epicureans and Stoics, alone of ancient sects, are mentioned in Acts of the Apostles 17:18. This allusion both prepares the reader for the Pauline citations to follow and places Christianity in historical confrontation with ancient philosophy. Vegio had attacked the republican fortitude of Roman heroes; Antonio now lauds the tribulations of martyrs in the service of what Valla calls the "Christian republic" (pp. 2, 126). The shift in viewpoint from pagan to Christian which is implicit in the allusion to Acts of the Apostles—Paul quotes from both the Psalms and Aratus—is reflected in Antonio's combination of classical and Biblical language, as well as in his comparison of Stoics to Pharisees and Epicureans to Sadducees (p. 109). Vegio's jesting allusion to the veiled Socrates of Plato's *Phaedrus* (p. 92) is replaced in Antonio's discourse by the image of Moses veiled as a symbol of divine allegory (p. 120). Antonio begins his exposition of celestial beatitude by denying the power of words to convey adequately the joys of salvation; in disclaiming his own ability, he praises Vegio's oratorical skill in moving and delighting:

> It is not enough to define and locate this good, unless we also explain as best we can its quality and quantity. A discourse which skims swiftly over its subject in a few words leaves the mind unmoved, for numerous points must be explained, elucidated, and illustrated, especially in an important discussion. Thus if Vegio in his defense of pleasure deemed necessary both to teach his audience how great a good pleasure is and to endeavor with great zeal to delight and move our minds to assent, does it not belong to the dignity of our doctrine, so to speak, to provide an advocate for the cause, neither omitting what must be said in praise of the perfect good nor leaving this venerable subject unhonored? (p. 116)

Antonio's discourse on the highest Christian good aims to move its hearers and above all, like Vegio's defense of pleasure, to delight them: Antonio intentionally passes over the medieval topics of earthly woes and infernal torments in order to deliver a panegyric on heavenly delights. Antonio explains his choice of this topic in terms of the psychology of reward asserted by Vegio in his refutation of Stoic virtue:

> Since I am speaking before you excellent and learned men, I shall pass over the topic of hell. Noble minds fear no laws and are not frightened by the prospect of torments, but are rather allured by rewards. It is of such rewards, those consisting in eternal pleasures, that I must speak according to my design, and I must show how greatly eternal pleasure surpasses terrestrial pleasures. Hear then my discourse on the rewards of Christians, in which I shall try to relate not what is trite and common but what is new (*nova dicere conabor*). (p. 118)[25]

Whereas in the classical arguments of the first part of his discourse Antonio dealt with the Stoic position of Catone, in his Christian panegyric he subtly adopts the themes of Vegio's Epicurean speech, raising terrestrial pleasures to celestial beatitudes (pp. 24, 123).[26]

The dialogue ends with a return to the temporal scene of the humanist circle as Guarino delivers his verdict on the speeches of Vegio and Antonio:

> Maffeo and Antonio both seemed to sing, as it were, most sweetly the praises of pleasure, but Maffeo may be likened most to a swallow, and Antonio to a nightingale . . . You are aware that the poets imagined these birds as sisters . . . and took them to signify oratory and poetry, which are sister arts . . . They considered the swallow like the eloquence of the city, exercised within the walls, in the court and in courtrooms: and they thought the nightingale like the eloquence of the woods and of the poets, who seek out the forests and solitary places frequented not by men but by the Muses. As much as the nightingale surpasses the swallow in singing by her power, sweetness, and variety, so much the poets said that their voices surpassed the orators and others.

Guarino says that the setting of the debate confirms his verdict: the garden of Book III, which Vegio had compared to the gardens of Epicurus, becomes a symbol of paradise:

> To prove my statement with a divine testimony (as the ancients would have called it), Vegio sang like a swallow under the colonnade, Antonio like a nightingale beneath these trees almost in the wood. Vegio sang by

day, but Antonio, following the nightingale's peculiar habit, sang after sunset. You may judge for yourselves, most learned men, if I speak falsely. You will certainly grant me this, and consider it a miracle: Vegio brought our bodies into this "paradise" (for so the Greeks call an orchard), but by speaking in this same paradise, Antonio bore our minds into another, more excellent paradise. Such is my verdict. (p. 137)

The dialogue thus ends with a second verdict which, unlike Antonio's pronouncement on Catone and Vegio, judges not the moral and philosophical validity of their positions but rather the effect of their eloquence. Guarino likens Antonio's celestial panegyric to poetry, thereby recalling the definition of poetry by Quintilian, who notes that poetry is "likened to the epideictic kind . . . and only seeks to give pleasure" (*Inst. orat.*, X, 1, 28). The notion of pleasure accordingly assumes a rhetorical dimension at the conclusion of *De vero falsoque bono*, and the superiority of Antonio's discourse is judged not by doctrinal criteria but by the measure of his psychagogic eloquence: "speaking in this paradise, Antonio bore our minds into another, more excellent paradise."

As Valla's revisions of his dialogue suggest, the specific setting of the work—originally the Roman Curia, then Pavia—is by no means as important as the setting of Bruni's *Dialogi* or of Poggio's *De avaritia*. Rather, the important element is Valla's "casting" of the interlocutors, on the model of Augustine's *Contra Academicos* and of Poggio's *De avaritia*, which reflects Valla's rhetorical conception of a forensic debate between contrasting philosophies and psychologies. Although the argument of the dialogue is developed according to the correspondence of style and temperament exhibited by the interlocutors, the social and historical elements of the discussion transcend its locality and moment and address larger questions than those in Poggio's *De avaritia*, its immediate predecessor.

Poggio's *De avaritia* had been specifically aimed at contemporary, especially clerical, avarice and at the inadequacies of contemporary preachers. Both targets of Poggio's polemics were readily identifiable from the beginning of the dialogue, in the discussion of Bernardino, and later in the explicit references to contemporary situations. In Valla's *De vero falsoque bono*, on the contrary, the discussion begins abruptly with a generalized lament on man's condition, and nearly all the argumentation depends on allusions to classical myths and examples suited to the universal nature of the topic. Even the final discourse of Antonio, who calls the interlocutors to an awareness of their Christian modernity, is remarkably detached from the contemporary setting.

Valla's *De vero falsoque bono* is a dialogue across centuries of historical thought, a synoptic examination of Western philosophy and morality that conflates disparate chronological elements. The ambiguous references to the *Stoici* and *philosophi* pose a particular problem in the interpretation of the dialogue. Catone's initial speech contains elements of Stoic idealism, of Aristotelian ethical doctrine, and of the medieval abhorrence of the present life; whereas, in Antonio's verdict, Boethius comes under attack as a Stoic and a dialectician. The term "Stoic" thus becomes a catch phrase for diverse philosophical and psychological attitudes. As Gerl has shown, the Stoicism attacked by Valla's Vegio represents various forms of abstract rationalism which argue about man's existence and nature from *a priori* principles and according to fixed rules of dialectic.[27] To this Stoicism Valla opposes what he calls Epicureanism, a similarly ambiguous classical term for a new humanist outlook. Valla's Epicureanism opposes Stoic abstract rationalism and its dialectical method by proposing an inductive empiricism which examines the lives and behavior of men by the practical and flexible methods of rhetoric.

The foundations for Valla's rhetorical dialogue had already been laid in Poggio's *De avaritia* by Loschi's arguments in favor of avarice, which maintained the acceptability of seeking wealth, citing numerous examples from contemporary practice. Instead of *a priori* deduction, such as that symbolized by the ancient etymology of the word *avarus*, Loschi employed inductive reasoning to argue that a notion related to avarice but without moral implications was natural and acceptable. As he asserted, "we must not regulate our lives by the standards of philosophy" (I. 16: *vita mortalium non est exigenda nobis ad stateram philosophiae*). The balance of philosophy (*statera philosophiae*) cited by Poggio's Loschi recalls Cicero's *De oratore* II, where Antonius evaluates the contribution of Greek philosophy to the orator's art, a passage that greatly influenced Valla. In discussing the philosophical embassy of Diogenes, Critolaus, and Carneades to Rome in 155 B.C., Antonius provides a comparative judgment of their three respective sects, the Stoics, the Peripatetics, and the Academics. He complains of the Stoics that their dialectic teaches only how to distinguish abstract problems and offers no point of contact with the orator's material for argument, the occurrences of daily life and individual circumstances. "For our speaking must be suited to the ears of many, delightful and persuasive in proving our points, which are weighed not in the goldsmith's balance, but in a sort of popular scale" (38, 159: *non aurificis statera, sed populari quadam trutina*). Antonius further observes that the Peripatetics are more useful (Aristotle had written practical books on rhetoric), while the marvelous eloquence of the Academic Carneades would be desirable in any orator (38, 160-161).

There can be little doubt that this passage from Cicero, which Valla also cites in his *Dialecticae disputationes,* influenced his selection of the Stoics as the object of his attack in *De vero falsoque bono,* for it identifies the Stoics as dialecticians and impugns their abstract logic as detached from the practical realities with which the orator must deal.[28] Cicero's critique of the style of the Stoics also raises a methodological objection against them. The Stoics, he notes (II, 38, 159-160), provide purely abstract principles of logic for judging the coherence of an argument, which are of no help in the concrete judgments required to begin an argument (*quem ad modum inveniam quid dicam*) and to reach a valid conclusion (*quo modo verum inveniatur*). In terms of Valla's realist notion of human ethics, in which rhetoric rather than philosophy must decide the truth, the Stoic dialecticians offer an abstract system of logical coherence, but they fail to establish its connection with the concrete realities of human behavior—the orator's domain—at either the beginning or the conclusion of an argument. Detached from the realm of practical experience, the philosophy of the Stoics—in the broadest sense in which Valla employs the word—is incapable of judging the realities of human behavior; it has therefore substituted a false ethical good, the abstraction *honestas,* for the true one, which Valla calls *voluptas.*

Vegio's doctrine of *voluptas* in *De vero falsoque bono* affirms the value of human experience over systems of abstract logic. His method of argumentation is accordingly rhetorical, that is, grounded in practical realities, in Ciceronian terms, with the practical aim of delighting and the practical effect of persuading. Indeed, the whole of Valla's dialogue tends to serve these rhetorical ends, and the author himself announces his sympathy with Vegio's position early in Book I by welcoming the new doctrine of pleasure as a refutation of Stoic abstractions (p. 22). For the same reason, Antonio in Book III alludes to Valla's *Dialecticae disputationes,* which demonstrate, as Vegio argued earlier, the superiority of rhetoric to dialectic (p. 113). Vegio's allusion to Carneades in his peroration (p. 89) restores a Ciceronian notion of discussion, since Cicero's Carneades is a model of rhetorical eloquence and persuasion, and it abrogates the Augustinian prohibition of Academic argument. At the same time, the allusion to Carneades reveals the actual view of the author who, though obliged to hide his opinion in the argument of the dialogue, in fact supports the doctrine of *voluptas* and strongly opposes the Stoics.

In establishing the notion of *voluptas* as an ethical good, Valla follows the humanist preference for experience over logic, which is dominant in the dialogue from Petrarch onward. Valla's dialogue also shares the tendency of the humanist dialogue to engage in covert polemics. There are several indications that the anti-Stoic arguments of the work are aimed not only at past philosophical figures and sects but also at contemporary groups and situations. When in replying to Catone, Vegio says that present-day philosophers call themselves guides of all others (p. 15), he clearly has in mind the theologians of the day. Whereas Bruni implicitly identified contemporary philosophers and theologians with Cicero's Stoics, Valla exploits the ambiguity of the classical terms *Stoici* and *philosophi*, as if intending to refute only ancient thinkers. While Vegio's assertions, like those of Niccoli in Bruni's *Dialogi*, are extenuated by professions of his insincerity, the end of Valla's dialogue does not present the same harmony as that depicted at the conclusion of Bruni's *Dialogus II*. Instead of being restored to the group as Niccoli had been, Vegio is dramatically isolated as a discordant element in the final scene. He observes that while Antonio's discourse may be reported by the others, he and Catone will perforce remain silent, for there are several counts against them (p. 138). But when Vegio offers to celebrate a nocturnal triumph in honor of Antonio's carrying the day in argument, his hedonistic proposal is rejected, and he is confined to his own house by decree of the others.

Bruni's *Dialogi* created an artful and artificial sense of reconciliation through the device of Niccoli's recantation. Bruni clearly perceived the danger of humanism's breaking too radically with traditional culture. Establishing this continuity was a central concern of his dialogue, as it would later be of Alberti's *Libri della Famiglia*. More detached from the local traditions, Poggio's *De avaritia* engaged past and present ecclesiastical authority polemically but still strove to incorporate Loschi in the group by questioning the sincerity of his defense of avarice and by recording his approval of the Christian homily of Andreas. Valla's *De vero falsoque bono* follows only in part the examples of Bruni and Poggio by calling in question Vegio's sincerity (pp. 106-107). But Valla is intent on urging the provocative novelty of his dialogue; the concluding discourses of Antonio and Guarino proclaim their own newness. At the conclusion of the dialogue, moreover, Vegio continues to act the part of the humorous Epicurean, as if to disprove Antonio's previous allegations of his insincerity in defending pleasure. Now unanimous in their admiration of Antonio's speech, the humanist circle is swift to ostracize the dissident Vegio, whose Epicurean proposals may be dangerous in public. Valla thus leaves the reader with a sense of unresolved tension that is peculiar both to the provocative design of his dialogue and to his own restless and polemical personality, which did not seek the tranquil resolution found in Bruni and Poggio.

The end of Valla's dialogue suggests, however, that the Christian teaching of Antonio has been welcomed by the humanist gathering as a higher form of the *voluptas* praised by the dissident Vegio. Antonio's discourse adopts Vegio's assertion of pleasure as man's concrete ethical goal but raises the notion of pleasure from terrestrial delights to celestial beatitude, clearly distinguishing earthly and heavenly goods (p. 110), according to the dichotomy formulated by Valla in the opening sentence of his proem to Book I. As Antonio's ethical good elevates the good advanced by Vegio, so the rhetorical persuasion of Antonio's panegyric of salvation seeks a higher poetic plane than that of Vegio's brash encomium of pleasure. As Guarino's verdict indicates, both Vegio and Antonio define and describe the *voluptas* which constitutes man's highest good on earth and in heaven, but Antonio's poetical discourse, a pious Platonic myth pregnant with scriptural metaphors and symbols, moves its hearers by a more spiritual persuasion.

The consensus of the group to Antonio's discourse, as well as the subsequent isolation of Vegio, create an artificial illusion of harmony which, as in Bruni and Poggio, is not strictly historical. The theological application of a poetical oratory was not likely to be accepted by either the clergy or the humanists of Valla's day. By assigning the longest part of the dialogue to Vegio and by isolating him as a dissident, Valla distracts the reader's attention from the boldest innovation of his dialogue, the merging of theology and rhetoric, which exactly reverses the Augustinian progression from rhetoric to philosophy to theology.[29] In comparing Vegio's urban Muses with Antonio's rustic Muse, Guarino's verdict runs directly counter to Augustine's condemnation of eloquence in his *Confessions*, where the elegance or inelegance of style is declared indifferent to salvation, just as nourishing food may be served in both urban and rustic dishware (V, 6, 10). The inclusion of theology in the work not only displeased religious authorities but also found little approval in the judgment of a humanist as celebrated as Bruni. In a letter of 1433 to Valla, Bruni refuses to offer his opinion on the question of man's ethical good in a future life, coldly observing that man ceases to be at his death.[30] Yet the conclusion of Valla's dialogue confidently portrays the felicitous union of rhetoric and theology which is eagerly welcomed by the group.

V

Leon Battista Alberti and the Volgare Dialogue

Pay heed, Battista and Carlo; it is for you, and not for our learned Lionardo, that I recount these principles drawn from the sources of the philosophers.

THE PROFOUND TENSION between the individual and society which characterizes the moral reflections of Leon Battista Alberti (1404-1472) finds literary expression in the dramatic ambiguities of the dialogue. Generally considered, Alberti's numerous dialogues reflect the influence of two separate classical traditions, according to their author's purpose and intended readership. With the sole exception of the Platonic inquiry *Pontifex* (1437), Alberti's Latin dialogues—the early *Intercoenales* (1430-1440) and the mature *Momus* (1443)—develop from a Lucianic inspiration, reflecting his predilection for allegories and apologues, and were intended for the amusement of a learned audience. Alberti's major Italian dialogues—the *Libri della Famiglia* (1433-1434, 1437), *Theogenius* (1438-1441), *Profugiorum ab aerumna libri* (1441-1442), and *De Iciarchia* (1470)—follow the Ciceronian model and seek rather to instruct a less cultivated public than to entertain an erudite minority.[1] Alberti's *volgare* dialogues reveal the same moral concerns and the same enthusiasm for discussion as those of Bruni, Poggio, and Valla: they likewise examine traditional problems of belief and behavior in the light of both classical learning and contemporary experience.[2] This continuity of the Ciceronian model is not surprising, for Alberti composed the first three books of *Libri Della Famiglia*, his first Italian dialogue, while he was employed in the Roman Curia, the setting of

Poggio's *De avaritia* and Valla's *De voluptate*. Yet significant differences in form, method, and setting distinguish Alberti's *volgare* dialogues from their Latin counterparts.

Alberti's choice of Italian as the language of his neo-Ciceronian dialogues places him outside the mainstream of Quattrocento humanist dialogues, but parallel to it. For the selection of the *volgare*, as Alberti explains in his proem to Book III of *Libri della Famiglia*, represents a conscious decision to write for a wider public than the few *litterati* who constituted the Latin readership of the day (I, 155-156). In so doing, Alberti proposes to follow the example of the ancient Romans, whose use of Latin was not the privilege of an educated minority. Alberti's dialogues resemble those of Cicero in expounding philosophical teachings otherwise unavailable to a larger public. As Cicero had composed Latin dialogues to explain Greek thought to his fellow Romans, so Alberti wrote his *volgare* dialogues as compendia of classical doctrines not accessible to contemporaries ignorant of Latin. The readership Alberti seeks to benefit is not the small circle of humanists for whom the dialogues of Poggio and Valla were intended. In their close adaptation of the Ciceronian model and in their treatment of secular problems, Alberti's Italian dialogues resemble more closely Bruni's *Dialogi*, to which they are also related by their Florentine heritage and consanguinity. The burden of the Latin and hence Christian tradition of the philosophical dialogue—so onerous a yoke to the restless spirit of a Poggio or a Valla—though weighing more lightly on the shoulders of a Bruni, was entirely cast off by Alberti when he chose the vernacular as the language of his dialogues.

The Latin dialogue, however, found a language ready-made, albeit in need of reform, for its philosophical purposes. Alberti's Italian dialogues, in contrast, have only partly assimilated their linguistic and formal classical models and are often couched in a ponderous style of Latinate neologisms and lapidary utterances. The linguistic polarity between Latinism and Tuscanism, which results in part from the tension between written and spoken Italian in the Quattrocento, also reflects a thematic polarity in Alberti's thought.[3] His moral writings vacillate between idealism and reality, between the teachings of classical authors and the vicissitudes of contemporary experience which, like the linguistic tension between Latin and Italian, seldom find harmonious resolution. The vigor of Albertian dialogue consists in the interaction of polarities which is generally expressed in the opposition of two interlocutors, whose differences on such antithetical themes as virtue and fortune, or doctrine and experience, motivate and articulate the discussion. In his ideal of the *ragionamento domes-*

tico, or "household discussion," Alberti seeks a stylistic, methodological, and social middle ground between the idealism of classical learning and the realities of contemporary experience. Although the clashes of argument found in Bruni, Poggio, and Valla are foreign to the subdued discussion of Alberti's *volgare* dialogues, in which a more Ciceronian tone of *humanitas* prevails, his dialogues reveal an underlying tone of doubt and perplexity which is more disturbing than the contradictions apparently resolved in the dialogues of the Latin humanists.

The *Libri della Famiglia* are not only Alberti's first but also his greatest achievement among his *volgare* dialogues. Originally composed in three books, with a fourth book added three years later, the *Libri della Famiglia* portray the discussions held in a gathering of the Alberti family in Padua in 1421, when the author's father Lorenzo lay on his deathbed. The setting reflects the exile of the family from their native Florence (1377-1428), a fact often mentioned in the discussion. The domestic and testamentary nature of the occasion gives rise in the first three books to conversations on family matters, while in Book IV the topic of friendship is discussed. Alberti introduces the work with a prologue addressed to his young kinsmen which explains that the dialogue will portray the distinguished members of the Alberti family providing useful precepts for the family's continued prosperity.

Book I begins with an affectionate address by Lorenzo to his sons Battista and Carlo, exhorting them to obedience to their elders, especially their adoptive parents Adovardo and Lionardo, and to the pursuit of virtue (I, 16-27). The two youths in fact remain silent throughout the book. When Lorenzo is counseled to rest a while, Adovardo and Lionardo begin to talk, marveling at the great affection of Lorenzo for his children (I, 27-30). The bachelor Lionardo raises the question whether the duties of fatherhood involve more care than contentment, to which the pessimistic and experienced father Adovardo replies that care prevails, initiating a discussion of the rearing and education of children. Lionardo asserts that the pleasures of fatherhood outnumber its cares, and the subsequent discussion is enlivened by the opposition between Adovardo's experienced pessimism and Lionardo's lettered optimism. At the end of the book, Adovardo concedes that diligent fathers do take pleasure in raising their children, and Lionardo humorously observes that now he must marry, in accordance with Adovardo's wishes, since no objection to married life remains.

In Book II Lionardo, who remains alone with Battista and Carlo, asks the boys their opinion of the preceding discussion. Having expressed his admiration of the numerous topics dealt with, Battista solicits Lionardo's opinion of Adovardo. Lionardo attributes Adovardo's fatherly concern to the loss of his brothers, and he asserts that friendship is the highest form of human affection. At this, Battista proposes a debate in which he will maintain the superiority of love to friendship. The ensuing discussion serves as a brief introduction to an extended disquisition of Lionardo on the selection of a wife and the increase of the family (I, 86-151).

After Alberti's proem on his choice of the vernacular, Book III opens on the next day with the arrival of the aged merchant Giannozzo. A discussion of household economy, arising from Giannozzo's reminiscences of his youth, is promoted by Lionardo so that Battista and Carlo may learn to become good householders and husbands. After Giannozzo's account of the "domestication" of his wife, which is in large part an adaptation of Xenophon's *Oeconomicus*, Adovardo joins the group (I, 216-243). Himself an experienced householder, Adovardo differs with Giannozzo on a financial question, and the discussion becomes a lively debate over problems of domestic management. On being summoned to attend to his own affairs, Giannozzo leaves, after exhorting the youths to economic caution and moral circumspection which will ensure their happiness.

The fourth book begins festively after dinner with the jests and recollections of the aged servant Buto, who greets the newly arrived Alberti elders. Buto recalls the domestic discussions of the previous generation of Albertis, whose learning had failed to teach them that wealth is more useful than any precept in cultivating friendships (I, 264). Buto's remark occasions an autobiographical narrative by Piero Alberti, who, having lost his landed property in the family's exile, had resorted to the service of three potentates: Duke Giangaleazzo Visconti of Milan, King Ladislaus of Naples, and anti-Pope John XXIII in Bologna (I, 265-283). The group then rises from the table, and the boys Battista and Carlo join Adovardo and Lionardo, who continue the discussion of friendship begun by Piero's personal history. Adovardo complains that classical treatises on the topic do not sufficiently prepare one to meet all the practical difficulties of contracting and maintaining friendships; Lionardo prevails upon him to expound his views, which he does in a discourse intended to instruct Battista and Carlo (I, 292-341). The work ends abruptly when the arrival of another Alberti kinsman is announced.

The predominant models for Alberti's *Libri della Famiglia* were Cicero's *De oratore, De senectute,* and *De amicitia*. Above all, *De oratore* served as a model for composing a dialogue as an extended discussion of an ethical ideal rather than as a debate of theoretical positions or a provocative treatment of controversial subjects like avarice or pleasure.[4] The brief and essaylike dialogues *De senectute* and *De amicitia* provide the instructive discourse of a revered elder in the presence of younger men, exemplifying the household discussion imitated by Alberti. These three dialogues of Cicero would have attracted Alberti as representations of the dignity and authority of past generations. In them Cicero did not, as he did in his philosphical dialogues, portray himself and his contemporaries, but he created an ideal picture of great Romans from the preceding century. Similarly Alberti, while employed in the Roman Curia, chose in the *Libri della Famiglia* not to represent the humanist circle of his colleagues but to portray the previous generations of his distinguished kinsmen.

Announcing the domestic topics of the first three books, Alberti's prologue to the *Libri della Famiglia* recalls both stylistically and thematically the beginning of Cicero's *De oratore*. The opening period—"Recalling to mind . . .I often used to wonder and grieve" (I, 3: *Repetendo a memoria. . . solea spesso fra me maravigliarmi e dolermi*)—reveals a Ciceronian influence both in its participial construction and in its Latinate vocabulary.[5] More significantly, Alberti's exposition of his topic imitates Cicero's method of anticipating in a preface the themes of the discussion to follow. In *De oratore,* Cicero reflects on the position of oratory among the arts, wondering at the paucity of excellent orators, and concludes that oratory embraces all the other arts (I, 2, 6-3, 11; 5, 16-6, 20). Alberti begins his prologue by questioning the power of fortune to render prosperous families miserable and, citing the example of his own family, asserts the supremacy of virtue over fortune (I, 3-8). In both Cicero and Alberti, the author's general thesis pervades the discussion of the dialogue and is intended as a practical exhortation both to the youths present and to the readers. The hortatory aspect of the dialogue—Cicero's encouragement to the pursuit of eloquence and Alberti's injunctions to virtuous economy—is reflected in the emphasis placed on the interlocutors' authority, which enhances the persuasiveness of the dialogue. Cicero professes to offer his readers no mere manual of Greek precepts but rather a compendium of the approved opinions of distinguished Roman orators (I, 6, 23). Alberti confirms the value of classical precepts by portraying the worthy example of family discussions (I, 10).

The prefatory remarks of Cicero and Alberti not only introduce the ideal conception of the topics to be discussed—the cultural supremacy of oratory and the ethical supremacy of virtue—but they also suggest the identification of the author's viewpoint with one of the interlocutors. In *De oratore*, the difference of opinion between Cicero and his brother Quintus foreshadows the positions of Crassus and Antonius in the discussion of Book I (2, 5). Likewise, Alberti's assertion of the supremacy of virtue anticipates the moral testament of his father Lorenzo in Book I of *Libri della Famiglia*. Yet Cicero establishes a conflict of opinion whereas Alberti insists emphatically on an absolute faith in virtue and removes Lorenzo from the subsequent discussion as an ideal point of moral reference. This faith in virtue is shared in Book I of *Libri della Famiglia* by Lionardo, who represents the optimistic humanism of Alberti's exhortations to his younger kinsmen, just as Adovardo expresses Alberti's private and profounder doubts.

Valla's *De vero falsoque bono*, which Alberti may have known in its early version *De voluptate*, established the psychological basis of dialogue by indicating the correspondence between the temperaments and philosophies of the severe Stoic Catone and the jesting Epicurean Vegio. Alberti's dialogues display a similar tension between the conflicting temperaments of Lionardo and Adovardo. The distinguishing feature of Albertian dialogue is the personal and introspective nature of such conflicts, which generally reflect tensions within the author's own personality.[6] Occasionally Albertian interlocutors, such as Giannozzo and Piero in *Libri della Famiglia*, display the strong outlines of individuality; but in general the polarity of Alberti's dialogues, typified by the difference between Lionardo and Adovardo in Book I, represents the inner conflict of the author's own vacillations. This conflict recalls the introspective drama of Petrarch's *Secretum*, in which similar tensions had first constituted a humanist dialogue of profound psychological oppositions. Although the troubled meditations of Petrarch's *Secretum* are far removed from the family conversations of Alberti's *Libri della Famiglia*, both dialogues bear the peculiar stamp of the author's personality in the diverse attitudes of the interlocutors.

Each book of *Libri della Famiglia* moves from an initial diversity of viewpoints toward a conclusion acceptable to the group. In Book I, a discussion of education takes place between the older Adovardo and Lionardo, whose differing attitudes and experiences continually enliven the work until they reach apparent agreement at the end (I, 80). Their disagreement recalls Book I of Cicero's *De oratore* with its differences of opinion between Crassus and Antonius, which were resolved in the second book by the latter's recantation.

In Book II of *Libri della Famiglia*, the young Battista challenges

Lionardo in a brief debate, and the two engage in an artificial exchange of arguments about the relative merits of love and friendship. The rhetorical exercise of their debate, which Lionardo calls a debate (*disputazione*) rather than a discussion (*ragionamento*), is reminiscent of Salutati's exhortation to debate in Bruni's *Dialogus I*; thus Lionardo encourages the young Battista to argue for the sake of the beneficial effects of exercising one's mind in debate.[7] When the debate is over, Battista agrees to listen attentively to Lionardo's exposition of precepts on domestic topics such as the selection of a wife; and the humanist spirit of discussion yields to the familial obedience required for the domestic instruction of the boys.

In Book III of *Libri della Famiglia*, the arrival of the aged householder Giannozzo shifts the level of discussion. Battista in Book II had promoted Lionardo's exposition with questions and comments; now it is Lionardo who encourages Giannozzo to relate his experiences in domestic economy. Only when the experienced Adovardo, who is older than Lionardo, returns to the discussion does the spirit of debate revive. At the conclusion of Book III, Giannozzo's prognostication of the youths' future happiness echoes the exhortation of Lorenzo in Book I and gives a thematic unity to the original three books.[8]

Book IV of *Libri della Famiglia*, which deals with the larger topic of friendship, lacks a close connection to the three earlier books. At the beginning of Book IV, the formerly prevalent tone of solicitude for the ailing Lorenzo is missing; rather, the number of interlocutors and an explicit allusion to ancient symposia create a festive scene. The larger gathering soon disperses, however, and after Piero's autobiographical account of his sojourns in Milan, Naples, and Bologna, Adovardo and Lionardo discuss friendship in the presence of Battista and Carlo. Adovardo's initial reservations about the utility of classical doctrines give place to an exposition of friendship illustrated with examples from antiquity.

In each book of Alberti's *Libri della Famiglia* there is a general movement from a conflict of viewpoints toward a continuous exposition acceptable to the group, who seek the moral edification of the youths. This articulation of the dialogue, beginning with debate and proceeding to uninterrupted speeches, follows the Ciceronian model of *Tusculanae disputationes* and *De finibus*. Ciceronian as well is the establishment of polarity between two speakers—Adovardo against Lionardo, Lionardo against Battista, and Giannozzo against Adovardo—although the debate is never so nicely balanced as Cicero's speeches *in utramque partem*. Albertian debates usually reflect a hierarchy of obedience within the family, according to which younger members of the family do not challenge their elders. Thus, Lionardo defers to the aged Giannozzo, while the older Adovardo questions Giannozzo in a critical manner. Yet the prevalent concern of all the elder Albertis for instructing the youths Battista and Carlo inevitably shifts the discussion from debate to exposition.

The movement from debate toward exposition reflects the didactic purpose of the *Libri della Famiglia,* which Alberti dedicates in his prologue to his young kinsmen (I, 12: *voi giovani Alberti*). This aim of educating the young, which results in almost continuous exposition, distinguishes Alberti's *volgare* dialogues from the Latin dialogues of Poggio and Valla and links them to the Ciceronian model of an experienced generation which instructs the young. In Cicero's *De oratore,* for example, Crassus and Antonius discuss the qualities of the orator for the benefit of the younger Sulpicius and Cotta, who are students of oratory. In Alberti's *Libri della Famiglia,* Battista and Carlo resemble Sulpicius and Cotta, although the Alberti youths participate less in the discussion.[9] The general silence of Battista and Carlo is in part prescribed by Lorenzo's teaching of obedience at the beginning of Book I, where he cites his own acts of respect to his elders as a "domestic example" for his sons (I, 23).[10] Whereas Sulpicius and Cotta are not excluded by their youth from the discussion in *De oratore,* Lorenzo's discourse tends to deny the possibility of debate between generations. The individual books of *Libri della Famiglia* accordingly present debates between the elders or instructive discourses for Battista and Carlo. Lorenzo's uncontested formulations of Stoic idealism are invoked repeatedly later by the Alberti elders (I, 43, 75, 80, 108, 129), and the obedience of Battista and Carlo is symbolized by their dutiful attentions to their father Lorenzo, which frequently interrupt and articulate the discussion (I, 81, 128, 243, 283).

The discourse of Lorenzo represents the vanishing point, as it were, of Albertian dialogue, which tends to become a didactic exposition delivered by a venerable elder to obedient and silent youths. This form typifies Alberti's later *volgare* dialogues, as well as Palmieri's *Vita civile.* Much of the inspiration for Lorenzo's discourse—especially the words quoted from his own father, Benedetto Alberti (I, 17-20)—derives from Cicero's *De senectute,* which with its companion piece *De amicitia* is fundamental to Alberti's *Libri della Famiglia.*[11] In his preface to *De senectute,* Cicero emphasizes the dignified authority of the principal speaker, Cato, and he contrasts his historical interlocutors to the mythological characters in the dialogue-fables of Ariston of Ceos (1, 3). Alberti himself wrote such fables in Latin—*Philodoxeos* (1425), *Intercoenales,* and *Momus*—for the entertainment of a learned readership. In his *De amicitia* as well, Cicero describes the principal interlocutor Laelius as ideally suited to discuss friendship, because discourses are lent gravity by the authority of past generations (1, 4). In the same fashion, Alberti in his prologue commends the authority of former generations of Albertis (I, 10: *nostri passati Alberti*); and his selection of the preceding generation as interlocutors in *Libri della Famiglia* enhances the persuasive force of its precepts (I, 10-12).

Alberti's use of Cicero's *De senectute* provides a key to understanding the peculiar tensions of the *Libri della Famiglia.* The influence of *De senectute* is apparent in the speech of Lorenzo and in his evocation of his father Benedetto; the figure of Giannozzo in Book III also recalls the aged Cato of Cicero's dialogue. In the idealized world of *Libri della Famiglia,* Alberti has adapted many of the themes suggested by his Ciceronian model. Before writing the *Libri della Famiglia,* he had already used *De senectute* as a source for his early essay *De commodis litterarum atque incommodis* (1430), but in that work Cicero provided a negative model for arguments which Alberti reverses. Cicero's dialogue refuted the alleged disadvantages of old age—that old men are infirm, enjoy no pleasures, and play no part in affairs—by adducing examples of the vigorous longevity, the moderate pleasures, and the high offices and authority enjoyed by old men. Alberti's essay, on the contrary, examines the possible rewards of literary studies and concludes that the endless lucubrations of scholars render them infirm, preclude their enjoyment of pleasure, and deny them participation in public and commercial affairs. Alberti's *Libri della Famiglia* then open the cloistered vision of his *De commodis* to the broader prospects of domestic affairs and public life, deriving positive inspiration from Cicero's dialogue-essay on old age. Alberti considers the individual a part of his family and society, and no longer the isolated student of the earlier essay.

As attentive and generally silent auditors, Battista and Carlo in *Libri della Famiglia* recall not only Scipio and Laelius in Cicero's *De senectute* but also the young men Fannius and Scaevola in *De amicitia.* The setting of *De amicitia* provided a model for the dialogue as a family discussion, for Fannius and Scaevola are the sons-in-law of the elderly Laelius, whose exhortations to the two youths anticipate the hortatory vocative "Battista e tu Carlo" of Alberti's interlocutors.[12] The eagerness of Fannius and Scaevola, moreover, in promoting Laelius' discourse served as a model for the obedient role of Battista and Carlo in the *Libri della Famiglia.*[13]

Alberti's imitation of Cicero's dialogues on the orator, on old age, and on friendship in part reflects his selection of a topic requiring ideal description rather than antithetical debate and in part suggests his own preference for earlier authoritative figures as distinguished interlocutors in an elevated discussion. In Alberti's *Libri della Famiglia,* the disagreements and debates between elders of different temperaments and experience serve to articulate the didactic expositions offered to Battista and Carlo. The discussion is governed by a familial decorum of deference to age, established early in the work when Lorenzo is first addressed by Adovardo, "who was older than Lionardo" (I, 14). As in Cicero's ideal dialogues, the young interlocutors encourage their elders, who always speak with a view toward edifying their youthful auditors.

The deference to age represented in *Libri della Famiglia* reflects the value accorded by the Alberti men of affairs to years of experience, as Lorenzo indicates in recounting his father Benedetto's praise of old men (I, 17-21). Yet the only characters continually present in the dialogue are the inexperienced youths Battista and Carlo and the bookish bachelor Lionardo. The boys are generally silent, and Lionardo plays the major role, unifying the work by his presence. In the first two books, he speaks of individual aspects of family life—education and marriage—in a learned tone which betrays the optimism of inexperience. In the last two books, the discussion shifts to topics of wider scope—marital relations, business ties, and friendship—and is entrusted to men of experience like Giannozzo and Adovardo, while Lionardo merely promotes their discourses. The *Libri della Famiglia* thus depict the confrontation of the new humanist learning, represented by Lionardo, with various aspects of human society viewed more widely. The limitations of inexperienced learning are gradually demonstrated, as Lionardo's erudite notions about the individual yield to the discourses of more experienced men—both the lettered Adovardo and the unlettered Giannozzo—concerning the larger problems of life and society.

Albertian dialogue is articulated by the alternation of learned optimism and experienced pessimism. Alberti's early Latin essay *De commodis,* dedicated to his brother Carlo, had warned young scholars not to expect material benefits from study and had urged the Stoic ideal of a wisdom disdainful of practical rewards. The mercantile ethic of *Libri della Famiglia* seeks to foster the financial prosperity denied the scholar of *De commodis,* but an underlying tension remains between the ideal learning expounded and the hardships of reality experienced by the interlocutors. In Books I and IV, Lionardo's faith in classical learning is repeatedly challenged by

Adovardo; in Books III and IV, Giannozzo, Piero, and the servant Buto all display an ironic reserve concerning the value of learned discussion. Despite the ideal terms of the discussion, the most lively contests arise over purely financial questions (I, 79, 246, 264-265). The economic catastrophe of the Alberti exile has left a strong mark on the tone and temperament of the interlocutors.

A similar tension is found in Alberti's later *volgare* dialogues, which tend, however, to assume the form of treatiselike compendia, with few vivid exchanges of conversation. In *Theogenius, Profugiorum,* and *De Iciarchia,* the tension is less sharply defined than in the *Libri della Famiglia,* where the contrast between men of learning and men of experience is more dramatic. The tension of the later dialogues lies rather in the recognition of the limited power of moral doctrines to ensure happiness. This discrepancy is already present in Adovardo's pessimistic critique of classical precepts on friendship in Book IV of *Libri della Famiglia.* Adovardo laments the insufficiency of ancient treatises to prepare one for the vast uncertainties of human life (I, 284-287). Although he affirms the value of classical learning, he maintains that it is impossible to foresee and remedy every situation by the learning which books afford (I, 291-292).

The method of Alberti's *volgare* dialogues consists in part of contrasting high intellectual and moral aspirations to the emotional and physical hardships of reality. In *Theogenius* (II, 66), the haughty Tichipedo mocks the vigils and infirmities of the recluse scholar Teogenio in a speech that recalls the description of student misery in Alberti's *De commodis.*[14] Not even Teogenio's devoted pupil Microtiro finds his moral counsel sufficient to cancel the memory of his numerous misfortunes (II, 96). Similarly, when Agnolo Pandolfini repeatedly asserts the utility of his precepts in *Profugiorum,* he is challenged by the doubts of Niccola de' Medici, who questions the power of moral conviction to control the emotions and impugns the moral integrity of the ancient philosophers whose lives belied their teachings (II, 114-115, 117-118, 163). In *De Iciarchia,* the aged Battista's didactic expositions are twice interrupted by the reservations of Paulo Niccolini who, like Adovardo in *Libri della Famiglia,* knows from experience as a father the practical difficulties of achieving excellence (II, 211, 270). Alberti's later dialogues consist largely of moral disquisitions, and their constitution as dialogues is necessary in order to test moral doctrines by contemporary experience and to allow objections to idealism detached from reality.

At the end of Book I of *Libri della Famiglia,* Adovardo begs Lionardo not to play the Stoic with him (I, 80: *Or ben, Lionardo, non m'essere testé meco così in tutto stoico*). Adovardo's objection to Lionardo's lofty moralizing continues the emphasis on practical reality which characterizes the moral teaching of humanist dialogues from Petrarch onward. Because of their secular nature, Alberti's *volgare* dialogues protest less against the rigid absolutism of theology in the Scholastic tradition than against the abstract idealism of humanist learning. The criterion of experience is fundamental in examining moral questions, and the elevated doctrines of classical authors are tempered by the common sense that experience provides, as in the dialogues of Poggio and Valla. The spirit of Alberti's dialogues is best exemplified by the practical Giannozzo and best formulated by the sage Adovardo, who observes that learning cannot be gained merely from the silent and solitary reading of books (I, 287: *Né puossi bene averne dottrina solo da' libri muti e oziosi*).

Experience teaches moderation, in accordance with the dictates of common sense, which constantly tests the validity of moral doctrines. The *Libri della Famiglia* exemplify the household discussion as an intellectual and social realization of Alberti's moral ideal of moderation.[15] The interlocutors of *Libri della Famiglia* conceive their household discussion as a mean between the ignorance of the masses and the subtleties of the humanists. This ideal is most clearly expressed by Lionardo, who in Book I confesses the limitations of his learning: "To the learned I could only relate what is already familiar to them, while the ignorant, I assure you, would think little of me and my opinions and would take little note. But those somewhat steeped in letters would wish to hear from me that ancient eloquence which was both polished and sweet" (I, 102).[16] Similarly, when Adovardo in Book IV doubts his ability to discuss friendship adequately, Lionardo encourages him to continue for the benefit of Battista and Carlo: "in these family discussions of ours, it will suffice to meet our own needs. Another time you may satisfy the masses and the learned" (I, 301).

The discussions of *Libri della Famiglia* permit occasional refinements in arguing a point. Thus in Book I Adovardo challenges Lionardo and compares himself to those who wish to excel in discussion by examining all the fine points (I, 61). But Lionardo replies that their private discussion does not require extreme logical accuracy: "Here between ourselves let us allow a freer conversation, not as carefully weighed or as definitely polished as others might wish. Ours has been a household's family discussion, not meant to teach you in what fields you are more expert and learned" (I, 62). In Book II Lionardo notes that a family discussion requires common sense rather than elegance: "Let us then return to our topic, which we shall discuss in as open and familiar a manner as possible, without any elegant or highly polished expression, since I think we require fine thoughts rather than a refined style of speaking" (I, 205).

The moral instruction which is the aim of the household discussion permits a certain freedom in expounding various topics, and Alberti's interlocutors insist on the free organization of their remarks. At the beginning of Book II of *Libri della Famiglia,* Battista marvels at the wide range of topics discussed in the conversation of Book I. Lionardo cites Cicero's *Orator* (16, 52) on the flexibility of discourse and insists that domestic discussion does not require the strictly logical exactitude and exhaustiveness of philosophical dispute.[17] Indeed, when Lionardo responds to Battista's arguments in favor of love, he professes to relate only what comes to mind, for he knows that Battista is not truly given to amorous passions (I, 93). In *Profugiorum,* Agnolo offers to reply to Niccola in an impromptu fashion, saying what comes to mind (II, 119). The same freedom in speaking is explicitly requested by the aged Battista of Book II of *De Iciarchia:* "From you, Paulo, and from you, Niccolò, both prudent men, I ask this license, that without establishing new principles or outlining a new order for this subject, I may (as I have done so far) only relate what comes to mind that is relevant to my purpose. It is not our aim to conduct a philosophical session with precision and circumspection. It will suffice if in these family discussions I imbue our minds and souls with excellent precepts for becoming outstanding men" (II, 219-220). Later in the same book, Battista denies the necessity of strict organization, adding (as Lionardo does in *Libri della Famiglia*) that worthy moral teaching pleases in any form: "I can well imagine that you expected a more precise order in my remarks. But as I spoke, it seemed to me that the thoughts that occurred to me were in themselves so valuable that they would greatly please you no matter how I expressed them" (II, 243). At the beginning of Book III, Battista clarifies the improvised order of his remarks with the help of a simile:

> As I have done so far, I shall now proceed from topic to topic, relating the sayings and precepts of ancient sages, and you will find delight and profit in hearing them even if I speak without order. The master builders of an aqueduct take care to determine the most suitable and unimpeded course for drawing off the water before they open its source. So in this naturally vast, grave, and diffuse material, I should have to arrange my discussion so that it would be not abrupt, disjointed, or confused, but conducted from topic to topic with pleasing aptness and ease. (II, 264-265)

In fact Battista does not "conduct" his discourse with such care and order. His image of the aqueduct recalls the opening scene of the dialogue, in which the Arno overflows its banks, suggesting Alberti's inability to control the flow of his ideas.[18]

There is a tension within the lengthy expositions of Alberti's interlocutors who, besides being challenged by the skepticism of experienced speakers, are also aware of their own shortcomings as moral preceptors. Attempting an eclectic synthesis of ancient ethical doctrines relevant to modern life, Alberti's didactic interlocutors often confess their difficulty in providing coherent moral teachings that will benefit their auditors. In Book II of *Libri della Famiglia,* Lionardo admits his doubts to Battista and Carlo: "I must warn you that these matters are vaster and more difficult to explain than you might think. They are found scattered and hidden, so to speak, amid the great abundance of various writers, so that to attempt to recount and order them all, putting them in their proper place, would be a laborious task for even a learned man. One would have first to review, reselect, and reorganize each part of the subject a great deal" (I, 101). Alberti's interlocutors conceive their teachings as a sort of physical arrangement of knowledge. Describing his difficulty in a typical Albertian simile, Lionardo voices sentiments that Alberti himself no doubt felt:[19]

> If I wished to expound these matters here in a confused manner, whoever should hear me would feel like travelers at daybreak. For those who on previous journeys have seen the countryside by day will recognize the place and its sights, and despite the darkness will perceive whether anything has changed. But those who have never seen the place in a better light will pass and wonder that so little can be discerned, having no clear impression of the site. Such would be the case with me . . . From the darkness of my dim memory, I might offer you some shadow of doctrines which are perfectly explained by others but unfamiliar to you and which I should make less clear. (I, 101)[20]

In *Theogenius,* Teogenio expresses the same doubts when faced with an abundance of classical arguments to cite to the troubled Microtiro: so many sayings of the ancient philosophers and poets occur to him that he doesn't know where to begin (II, 62). Likewise, in Book III of *Profugiorum,* Agnolo expresses dissatisfaction at having spoken without preparation. Like Lionardo in *Libri della Famiglia,* he resorts to a simile:

> I thought I had finished and completed my discussion, and I thought that nothing remained but the final epilogue and brief summation of the points I had made. But now I realize how wrong I was, and I wish I had not begun what I could not discuss in an orderly way. Nor do I now know in what

direction I should turn to proceed in the proper order. I may have said many useful things, but I feel like the man who found the tip of a large rock buried in his vineyard. He decided to dig it up, but later regretted the toil and time he lost over it, for he saw that it was larger than he had thought and less likely to be moved. (II, 160)

Despite the difficulties of providing relevant moral teaching from classical sources, Alberti's interlocutors discourse without rigid organization. Alberti's use of the dialogue represents a solution to the predicament of modern humanists, who seem condemned to the mere repetition of classical sources. Agnolo's humble simile of the rock is answered by Niccola's extended simile about the invention of the mosaic floor (II, 160-161).[21] After an ancient architect in Asia, Niccola explains, had finished the construction of a temple, he observed that the bare floor was not worthy of the splendid ornaments of the rest of the structure. In order to decorate the floor, he gathered up the tiny fragments of precious material that remained and arranged them together according to color and shape to form various pictures. The floor became as pleasing as the rest of the edifice. The same is the case, Niccola asserts, with today's humanists, who contemplate the marvelous edifice of ancient ethical teaching:

The men of genius in Asia and especially in Greece invented all the arts and sciences over the centuries, and constructed in their writings a sort of temple as a residence for Athena and for Providence, the goddess of the Stoics. They raised the walls with the investigation of truth and falsehood, placed the columns by discerning and noting the effects and forces of nature, and, to protect this great work from the buffets of adversity, they added a roof, which was the knowledge of avoiding evil, desiring and attaining the good, hating vice, and seeking and loving virtue. (II, 161)

Unlike the ancient architect, Niccola continues, modern *litterati* do not use extant fragments but quarry amid finished works, reducing them to pieces that they then reassemble in new structures: "Hence the saying arose: 'Nothing is said that has not been said before.' We find these literary bits cited by so many, used and scattered in so many writings, that whoever wishes to discuss them has no choice but to collect and sort and assemble them in a manner both different from the others and appropriate to his own work, as if consciously imitating the man who made the mosaic floor" (II, 161).[22] The analogy with Roman ruins is clear: Alberti witnessed and deplored the contemporary practice of demolishing ancient structures to provide building materials.

On the one hand, modern writers on moral topics are reduced to assembling classical precepts for their own purposes. This is Alberti's intention in composing his dialogues. As he says in the prologue to *Libri della Famiglia,* he has found many useful precepts in ancient authors which he has assembled in his dialogue for the benefit of his young kinsmen (I, 10). On the other hand, as Niccola explains (II, 161), there is creative novelty in assembling the fragments so that they form a coherent picture which delights and pleases. In praising Agnolo's discourse, Niccola implicitly approves Alberti's own undertaking and accomplishment in composing his dialogues:

> Who could be so fastidious that he would not approve and praise the man who devoted his industry and diligence to such a carefully constructed work? Thus we, Agnolo, who see gathered by you what was scattered and worn in other authors, and who hear so many various matters placed together, conjoined, inserted, and bordering each other—all corresponding to one tone, all equal to one level, all extended in one line, all conforming to one design—we not only cannot desire more, nor merely approve and praise you, but we must owe you all the more gratitude and merit. (II, 161-162)[23]

The simile of the mosaic suggests above all the eclecticism in Alberti's dialogues, and the vocabulary of design employed by Niccola implies an esthetic delight in the imaginative mosaic of conversation.[24] The implication of artistic creation betrays Alberti's attempt to compensate for the derivative nature of his dialogues by invoking an artistic novelty like that which he confidently proclaims in his *De pictura* (1435-1436). Although Alberti sees little possibility of originality in his moral writings and frequently cites the Terentian dictum that all has been said before, he nevertheless recognizes the novelty of Quattrocento achievements in the visual arts.[25] In *De pictura* he affirms the possibility of progress in terms derived from Cicero's *Brutus,* which Poggio also adopted in his dialogues.[26]

The full implications of the mosaic simile are not expressed by the mere notion of artistic arrangement, and in fact Alberti's later *volgare* dialogues often seem prolix and disorganized rather than ordered and coherent. The simile of the mosaic rather symbolizes the plight of the eclectic philosopher who attempts to provide moral teaching relevant to the problems of the day. The ancient inventor of the mosaic floor had worked from remnants of a completed structure, supplementing a finished design with an improvised addition. Alberti's dialogues likewise seek to supply what is wanting in classical moral writings, namely a firm grounding in reality as a basis for modern ethical discussion. Niccola describes the perfected temple of ancient philosophy, the shrine of wisdom and Stoic thought, but the reality of Alberti's day indicated that the passage of time had been no kinder to the philosophical constructions of antiquity than to their architectural counterparts. Like Alberti the architect, Alberti the moralist borrows classical elements in order to provide a synthesis appropriate to the needs of the Quattrocento. The eclectic classicism of Albertian architecture is matched by that of Alberti's dialogues.

The first humanist dialogue of the Quattrocento, Bruni's *Dialogus I,* had launched an attack against medieval ignorance by citing the vast number of classical works lost since the fall of Rome. Alberti's description of the ancient temple of philosophy implies a similar loss of the coherence and perfection of classical thought. The temple, as Niccola describes it (II, 161), consists of three parts, which correspond to the three traditional branches of classical philosophy. The walls symbolize logic ("the investigation of truth and falsehood"), the columns, the physical sciences ("the effects and forces of nature"), and the roof, ethics ("the knowledge of good and evil, virtue and vice"). As in a real structure, it is this last feature, the roof of ethics, which has suffered the greatest damage, leaving modern man unprotected against the vicissitudes of fortune. Indeed, the buffets of fortune (*le tempeste avverse*), which moral doctrines should ward off, provide the occasion of Alberti's dialogues. In his prologue to *Libri della Famiglia,* Alberti hints at the exile of his own family when he describes the decline of great houses in times of adversity (I, 3); and in his dedication of *Theogenius* to Leonello d'Este, he explains that the work was written as a consolation for his own adverse fortunes (II, 55).

Although some classical treatises on moral problems have survived, they are insufficient by themselves to ensure the happiness of people living in a modern world far different from classical antiquity. They serve rather to contribute precepts and examples to the ethical mosaic of Alberti's *volgare* dialogues, which examine moral questions of the family, as in *Libri della Famiglia* or *De Iciarchia,* and of the individual, as in *Theogenius* or *Profugiorum,* in the new context of Quattrocento experience. In their original versions, the moral treatises of classical authors may have satisfied the needs of ancient morality, but their inadequacy in the modern era requires a new evaluation in the Albertian setting of family discussion. In Book IV of *Libri della Famiglia,* for example, Adovardo complains that the few classical treatments of friendship are too theoretical and enunciate merely static principles (I, 284-286). The validity of Adovardo's complaint is confirmed by Piero Alberti's autobiographical account at the beginning of the book, which indicates the practical compromises required in courting the favor of Quattrocento princes.

In *Profugiorum,* Agnolo discusses the remedies for melancholy that he has learned from his own long experience with the emotion (II, 111). The "mosaic" of his discourse is praised by Niccola, who declares that it embraces topics treated by none of the ancients (II, 162: *comprendesti faccenda da niuno de' buoni antiqui prima attinta*). The originality admired by Niccola reveals the sense of innovation which characterizes the humanist dialogue. As in Poggio and Valla, this novelty consists in the re-examination of traditional ethical teachings according to the relative criteria of personal experience and contemporary practice.

Because they deal with such relative questions, Alberti's dialogues presuppose the freedom of assertion and judgment proclaimed in Poggio's dialogues. Significantly, the freedom essential to debate is asserted by the figure of Battista, the author's *persona* as a youth in *Libri della Famiglia* and as an elder in *De Iciarchia.* In Book II of *Libri della Famiglia,* Battista, in offering to debate Lionardo, notes that his arguments may be advanced more for the sake of exercise than to support his true opinion.[27] In *De Iciarchia,* the freedom of each to judge for himself is maintained by the aged Battista, who assures his auditors Niccolò Cerretani and Paulo Niccolini that they will decide whether his discussion agrees with their own opinions (II, 265: *Co' ragionamenti nostri quanto io satisfaccia a' pensieri vostri, Niccolò, e tu Paulo, el iudizio starà in voi*).

The typical setting of Albertian dialogue as a household discussion reflects Lionardo's emblematic observation in *Libri della Famiglia* that his remarks seek a middle ground between humanist erudition and the illiteracy or indifference of the masses (I, 102). Alberti's ideal portrait of his own family recalls the gatherings of Cicero's dialogues, in which moderation sets the tone of the conversation. In both cases, the interlocutors' learning is tempered and tested by their practical experience in affairs—the oratory and politics of Cicero's noble Romans, and the commerce of Alberti's venerable forebears. The leisure (*otium*) of discussion is a diversion from, and preparation for, the business (*negotium*) of daily life, and it forms part of a tradition traced back to earlier generations—Scipio and Laelius, and Benedetto and Niccolaio Alberti (I, 173, 264).[28] The family discussion of Alberti's *Libri della Famiglia* portrays an educated mercantile class, neither detached and intellectual like the secretaries of the Roman Curia nor limited and uncultivated like less prosperous families.[29] The nature of their learning is reflected in Alberti's prose style, which combines colloquial Italian with Latinate vocabulary and syntax, striving always for the clarity and intelligibility necessary to the diffusion of classical wisdom.

In following the model of Cicero's dialogues *De oratore, De senectute,* and *De amicitia,* Alberti has consciously evoked an earlier generation of his kinsmen in order to establish a clear continuity with his family tradition. As Bruni's *Dialogus I* had recorded the successive generations of Florentine humanism (Marsili, Salutati, Bruni), so Alberti in *Libri della Famiglia* traces the lineage of household discussion from his grandfather Benedetto, through his father Lorenzo, to himself and his brother Carlo. Unlike Poggio and Valla, Alberti seeks not to break with the past but rather to enrich the family patrimony of discussion with the new acquisitions of humanist learning. The analogy with his Ciceronian models is clear, for Cicero had likewise grafted the new learning of his day onto the venerable stock of earlier Roman generations. The linguistic anachronisms of both authors' dialogues confirm the analogy; both Cicero and Alberti present interlocutors of traditional education speaking the ornate language of the new eloquence.

Despite the sense of cultural continuity established by Alberti's *Libri della Famiglia,* in which the strident dissidence of Bruni's Niccoli would be inconceivable, the world of Albertian dialogue is curiously idealized and detached. Notwithstanding his ancestral attachments and the revocation of the family exile, Alberti spent little time in Florence. The humanism of Bruni reflected his dedication to the culture of his adopted homeland, and his Italian biographies of Dante and Petrarch in a sense continued the discussion of his *Dialogi.* Alberti, on the contrary, never mentions Dante, Petrarch, or Boccaccio in his writings; he clearly finds the predominantly commercial milieu of Florence uncongenial and, like his Florentine kinsmen, unresponsive to his literary efforts. In his essay *De commodis,* Alberti disaffectedly describes the Florentine passion for profit which he encountered on his first visit to the city.[30] This passage is echoed in Book I of *Libri della Famiglia* by Adovardo, who observes that children with literary ambitions are frustrated by the mercantilism of the Tuscan people, who are naturally and traditionally devoted to the incessant pursuit of gain (I, 41).

Adovardo's comment reveals the higher standards of Alberti's idealized interlocutors, who insist upon nobler goals than the mere acquisition of wealth. This idealism was evidently not shared by the actual members of the Alberti family who, as Alberti notes in his autobiography, scarcely deigned to read the headings of the various books of *Libri della Famiglia.*[31] When Lionardo in Book II remarks that the ignorant will take little note of his words (I, 102), he seems to have convicted the Alberti family—whether before or after the fact—of ignorance. There were other Florentines, however, who profited from Alberti's writings, deriving from them eloquent ornaments for their public speeches as well as inspiration for further study, and Alberti adopted these more studious fellow citizens as his spiritual kinsmen.[32] With the exception of the brief *Cena familiaris* (not certainly dated), Alberti's later *volgare* dialogues abandon the household setting of the Alberti family.

Although Adovardo's comment on the Florentine passion for gain reflects Alberti's disillusioned first impression of the city to which his family had been restored, the figure of the merchant Giannozzo in Books III and IV of *Libri della Famiglia* combines typically Florentine attitudes with the author's own moral strictures. Giannozzo is the caustic exponent of three overt polemics—against politicians, against the nobility, and against priests.

Giannozzo's denunciation of holding political office is directed only partially against the immorality of politicians (*statuali*) and represents rather the private merchant's abhorrence of time-wasting public office. Warning against the corruption and ambition of public service, Giannozzo counsels the moderate pursuit of private affairs, although he notes that the reasons for his attitude include personal disposition and the fact of the Alberti exile (I, 179-182). Responding to Giannozzo, Lionardo acknowledges the frequent enormity of Florentine ambition, attributing it to a libertarian tradition, as Alberti had in his *De commodis.*[33] Lionardo nevertheless urges the active participation of the citizen in public affairs if he is nobly motivated by honor, fame, and dignity (I, 183). If the Alberti family were recalled from exile, he surmises, it might regain its rightful place in the business of the republic (I, 185).

Giannozzo's animadversions on political offices reveal a disenchantment with the optimate government which had exiled the Albertis from Florence. When Giannozzo decries the self-seeking behavior of the nobility, he seems to speak for the collective opinion of the Alberti merchants as well as for the author (I, 251-253). Giannozzo's attack on the nobility reveals a mercantile attitude when he complains that the idle lords (*signori*) have no idea of how to earn a living and that what is lent them they throw away (I, 252). The saying of Antonio Alberti which Giannozzo cites to confirm his point—that the nobility insist on being greeted with words of gold—suggests the practical policy of the Alberti bankers, whose experience must have indicated the hazards of lending to princes.

Giannozzo's brief outburst in Book IV against the vices of the clergy assumes a more general tone and suggests the influence of Poggio's *De avaritia.* Like Poggio's Loschi, Giannozzo observes that all men are by nature inclined to pursue their own advantage (I, 282: *siamo quasi da natura tutti proclivi e inclinati all'utile*). Yet priests in particular are contentious and greedy, seeking to outdo one another, not in virtue or learning, but in ostentation and in the satisfaction of vicious appetites. Even here the mercantile note is struck, for Giannozzo adds that the clergy serve their own desires with no sense of thrift or economy (I, 282: *senza risparmio o masserizia*). As in his denunciations of politicians and the nobility, Giannozzo emphasizes as well the moral corruption of the clergy and its inevitable contagion.

These three instances of overt polemic define the social orientation of Albertian dialogue in a negative fashion. The ambiguity of Alberti's attitude toward political office, represented in the exchange between Giannozzo and Lionardo, appears in the vacillation of Alberti's later dialogues. A sense of withdrawal is dominant in *Theogenius* and *Profugiorum,* while *De Iciarchia* proposes the civic fruition of eloquence attained in private discussion.[34] Idle nobility and corrupt clergy arouse Alberti's humanist indignation, to which Giannozzo adds a note of mercantile disapprobation by deprecating unproductive sloth and vicious waste.

The mercantile attitudes of the interlocutors of *Libri della Famiglia*—Giannozzo's insistence on productive activity and Adovardo's pessimistic cautions against the vicissitudes of human life—distill the collective experience of the Alberti family and the personal experience of Alberti himself, who grew up in exile and was deprived of the advantages of his family's former prosperity. The nostalgic evocation of earlier generations of the Alberti family in the *Libri della Famiglia* suggests the cold reality of the family's decline, even after their return from exile.[35] Cicero, forced to retire from political life by the formation of the first triumvirate, had sought refuge in the creation of an ideal past in his dialogue *De oratore,* in which celebrated Romans discuss the orator's privilege which Cicero had once exercised. By the same token, when Alberti joined his family, newly restored to their native Florence, and met with disappointment, he found consolation in the dialogue portrait of an ideal family more receptive to the new learning than was his own. The *Libri della Famiglia,* constituting Alberti's literary tribute to his forebears, recalls the purpose of ancient Roman funeral laudations, which according to Cicero's *Brutus,* one of Alberti's favorite books, were intended to "embellish and preserve the memory of domestic glories and to celebrate the family's nobility."[36]

The world of Albertian dialogue is thus singularly idealized, reflecting the isolation of its author who, though employed in the Roman Curia and noted among its humanist members, turned to the tradition of his own family for an exemplar of learned discussion. Often his dialogues are more closely concerned with the practical necessities of economic life than were the debates of the Latin humanist dialogue. Alberti's choice of the Italian language testifies to his immediate purpose of reaching a large audience, although his generally Latinate style reveals an ideal and classicizing vision of the world. The *volgare* dialogues of Alberti realize his ideal of a mosaic of words and deeds both ancient and modern, possessing the grandeur of his neoclassical architecture.

VI

Giovanni Pontano and the Academic Gathering

Although I am old and weighed down with age, I am yet possessed of the hope that before I leave you I may see our Latin philosophy expounding its topics with a more refined style and elegance, and that abandoning this contentious manner of debating it may adopt a more tranquil form of speech and discussion, using its own proper and purely Roman vocabulary.

AMONG THE MOST original creations of Quattrocento literature, the five Latin dialogues of Giovanni Pontano (1429-1503) represent the confluence and the culmination of various Quattrocento dialogue traditions, and they point the way toward the dialogues of Erasmus in the next century.[1] Combining Platonic, Ciceronian, Lucianic, and symposiac elements, Pontano's dialogues present dramatically an allusive and often poetical evocation of the Neapolitan Academy during the latter half of the fifteenth century. Pontano's inventive delight in lyrical and comic interludes, as well as the corresponding poetic or colloquial shadings of a Latin rich in neologisms and nuances, transform the Renaissance dialogue into an imaginative work of art. At the same time, the learned gatherings portrayed in Pontano's dialogues continue the philosophical discussions of the early Quattrocento, now idealized and codified by the emergent classicism of the academy at Naples.

Whereas the early phase of the Quattrocento humanist dialogue revealed the predominance of the Ciceronian model, Pontano's first dialogues, *Charon* (1467-1470) and *Antonius* (1482-1490), contain numerous satirical episodes and encounters reminiscent of Lucian.[2] Yet the very first words of *Charon*—a philosophical exchange between the underworld judges Minos and Aeacus—indicate the pervasive influence of Cicero on the speculative discussions in these works. Adopting the Lucianic combination of philosophy and comedy, Pontano consistently alternates Ciceronian discussions with scenes of Lucianic satire.[3] Written at the midpoint of Pontano's literary career, the dialogue *Asinus* (1488-1492) constitutes a unique comedy, an autobiographical allegory of Pontano himself in an intermezzo-prologue to a philosophical discussion never recounted.[4] *Asinus* marks the transition from the Lucianic and satirical phase of Pontano's early dialogues to the Ciceronian and academic phase of his late dialogues. In the last two dialogues, *Actius* (1495-1499) and *Aegidius* (1501), the comic encounters of the early dialogues cease to interrupt the tranquil course of the discussions. The academy at Naples is presented as a sober symposium in which members discourse on varied topics and in which the ideals of Ciceronian classicism are never challenged. Whereas Pontano's early dialogues depicted an open circle in which the interlocutors engaged passersby in conversation and recounted contemporary controversies, the closed circle of the late dialogues finds recreation in the minutiae of grammatical problems and avoids direct confrontations with the outside world.

It is Pontano's last dialogue, *Aegidius*, which stands as the heir to, and the culmination of, the Quattrocento tradition of humanist dialogue. Composed a century after Bruni's *Dialogus I* had depicted the excitement of Florentine discussions, Pontano's *Aegidius* evokes a placid academic gathering in which the central themes of Quattrocento dialogues are strikingly recapitulated. As Pontano's literary and spiritual testament, *Aegidius* effects an apotheosis of classicism in an elevated gathering of the Neapolitan Academy. In a varied discussion, pregnant with symbols and syntheses, the dialogue seeks to reconcile the major forces at play in the earlier humanist dialogues of the Quattrocento. Sacred and secular become one in the new ideal of pious erudition, which Pontano calls his "Latin philosophy," a synthesis propounded as an "Augustinian" combination of religion and rhetoric, embracing Aristotelian philosophy and Ciceronian eloquence.[5]

Aegidius, which is set in Naples outside Pontano's house, begins with the arrival of two visitors, Suardino and Peto, who have come from Rome, traveling through southern Italy. Stopping before Pontano's house, the two travelers find this inscription on its walls:

FUTURE HEIR, SUCCESSOR, MASTER OF THIS HOUSE, FEEL NEITHER SHAME NOR GRIEF FOR ITS FORMER MASTER, WHO BUILT HIMSELF THIS HOME. HE CULTIVATED LETTERS, CULTIVATED THE NOBLER ARTS, AND CULTIVATED KINGS, HIMSELF

CULTIVATED BY HONEST YOUTHS AND HONEST ELDERS, WHO LAUDED HIS INTEGRITY, FAITH, AND GOOD MORALS. SUCH WAS GIOVIANO PONTANO, THE REMNANT OF AN EARLY AGE. HE LIVED FOR HIMSELF AND FOR THE MUSES. SO MAY YOU LIVE FOR YOURSELF AND FOR YOUR OWN, AND SO MAY YOUR CHILDREN ABOUND. BUT SHOULD YOU WRONGLY DAMAGE THIS STONE, MAY THE GODS BE ANGERED AGAINST YOU. (p. 245)

Coming out of his house, Pontano welcomes the pair and offers them refreshments from their journey (pp. 246-247). The atmosphere of learned hospitality and gaiety is briefly clouded when Pontano recalls the recent death of his lifelong companion, Pietro Compatre. He learns that Suardino and Peto too have reason to mourn the passing of a holy man, friar Mariano da Genazzano, general of the Augustinian order who "cultivated the Christian Muses" (pp. 247-248). Pontano urges the two to be consoled, for Mariano now enjoys celestial beatitude and has been succeeded on earth by Giles of Viterbo, the "Aegidius" of the dialogue's title, whom Mariano inspires through the "Christian Muses." Pontano recounts a sermon which Giles has recently preached before the people, an extended homily on John 14:6 ("I am the way, the truth, and the life") in which Giles denies that the ancients knew the true highest good of Christ (pp. 249-252). To his account of the sermon Pontano adds a recitation of a poem he has written on Mariano's death. He then expresses his own belief in a life after death, a personal faith confirmed by the universal belief in the soul's immortality, which has only recently been undermined by impious philosophers (pp. 252-254).

The opening scene of affectionate exchanges and fond recollections among Pontano, Suardino, and Peto serves as a prologue to the academic discussion which begins as other members of the academy appear.[6] The arrival of Francesco Pucci and Romano Tamira brings news of the vision seen by a monk at Monte Cassino, in which the late Gabriele Altilio, former bishop of Policastro and a member of the academy, rebuked his colleagues for engaging in vain pastimes and exhorted them rather to cultivate the "true Muses of piety and religion" (p. 256). Welcoming this pious "oracle" from his late friend, Pontano is moved to explain how God communicates with men, not through the inferior means of their bodies, but through their superior portion, the soul. In conclusion, Pontano adds his voice to Altilio's oracle, exhorting his colleagues to pursue piety and eloquence (pp. 257-259). Responding to Pontano's exhortation in a passage that recalls Bruni's *Dialogi*, Pucci ascribes the present decline of eloquence to the ignorant neglect of medieval theologians; but he expresses the hope, seconded by Tamira, that Pontano's studies and the new humanist translations from the Greek may restore ancient eloquence (pp. 259-260).

The custom of the academy requires the participation of all members present, and now that others have arrived, a series of discussions on various topics is begun.[7] The first man called upon to speak, Girolamo Carbone, quotes the opening of Virgil's fourth *Georgic* and asks Pucci and Tamira their opinions—or those of their teachers, Politian and Pomponio Leto—on the poetics of Virgilian exordia. Their proposed solutions to the problem are succeeded by Marino Tomacelli's request that Francesco Elio Marchese and Tristano Caracciolo compare the classical notion of the Elysian fields with the Christian doctrine of paradise. Their responses recall Book III of Valla's *De vero falsoque bono* in expounding the rewards of piety in the next life (pp. 265-266).

These learned exchanges invite Pontano's exclamation that Altilio's soul no doubt rejoices in the erudite piety of the academy. Such joy, he adds, might only be tempered by longing for the absent Sannazaro, who has followed the Aragonese king into voluntary exile at the French court (p. 266). As a "recreation" from the learned questions of the preceding discussion, Pietro Summonte describes Sannazaro's noble departure and recites the poet's valedictory elegiacs on Naples. Sannazaro's departure reminds Summonte of the recent death of Elisio Calenzio, whose piety in his final hour united him with Altilio in heaven (pp. 267-268).

After Pontano and Summonte have exchanged their sentiments of loss and recollection, the discussion returns to the consideration of learned questions. Chariteo reports his recent "conversion" from Platonic allegiance to Hermeticism and provides an exegesis of God's word as the source of creation, light, and man's salvation (pp. 268-271). The speech causes Giovanni Pardo to marvel that Chariteo risks provoking the natural scientists (*physici*) by such mystical speculation. With greater caution, Pardo limits his remarks to a discussion of the relative propriety of the Latin words *privatio* and *carentia* in denoting the Aristotelian principle of privation (pp. 271-273). Pardo then observes that Francesco Puderico too is at odds with scientists and astrologers, and he vindicates man's free will from the physical determinism of astrologers, asserting the superiority of man's spiritual portion to his natural elements, as Pontano had done before (pp. 273-279).

Pardo's discourse on free will moves Pontano to hope that in his lifetime he will witness the flourishing of a Latin philosophy. He is encouraged in this hope, he explains, by Giles of Viterbo who, responding to the inadequacies of medieval translations of Aristotle, has proposed several correct Latin equivalents for Greek philosophical terms. In order to illustrate the contemporary restoration of Latin philosophical vocabulary to its pristine propriety and elegance, Pontano relates Giles's recent discourse in the monastery gardens of San Giovanni a Carbonara (pp. 280-284). Concurring in Pontano's ideal and sharing his hope for a Latin philosophy, Suardino and Peto observe that the meetings of the academy contribute in no small part to this end. With the two travelers' promise to frequent the academy daily during their stay in Naples, the dialogue ends (p. 284).

The cumulative diversity of *Aegidius* is articulated by a number of verbal and thematic elements which unify the dialogue. The large number of interlocutors—twelve in all—and the variety of topics discussed recall the learned symposia of classical dialogue, but Pontano has lent a subtle unity to his work perhaps found elsewhere only in Plato's dialogues. Indeed, *Aegidius* seems to fuse the learned discourses of Plato's *Symposium* with the valedictory spirit of *Phaedo*.[8] Pontano's concern with succession—his lapidary inscription to the future inhabitant of his house, his discourse on the soul's immortality, and his praise of Pardo as likely successor to head the academy—reflects his spiritual preparation for death, in which he will join his friends Compatre, Altilio, Calenzio, and the holy friar Mariano. The central scene of the dialogue consists of an exchange between Pontano and his literary executor, Summonte, in which the exile of Sannazaro and the pious death of Calenzio are invoked as a culmination of the themes of loss and memory.

As in *Antonius*—Pontano's dialogue commemorating Antonio Beccadelli, founder of the academy—*Aegidius* is named for a person not present in the gathering, whose personality and thought nevertheless pervade the discussion. In his popular sermon and his private disquisition, the Augustinian friar Giles symbolizes the piety and erudition which are the ideals of Pontano's Latin philosophy, a synthesis of Aristotelian doctrine and Ciceronian eloquence. Through recurrent expressions of loss and affection, the dialogue weaves a fabric of past and future sodality in the figures of the aged Pontano and the young Giles.

As in Pontano's other dialogues, the underlying structural principle of the composition is symmetry.[9] In addition to pairing the interlocutors—Suardino and Peto, Pucci and Tamira, Marchese and Caracciolo—the scenes of the dialogue are arranged symmetrically around the central exchange between Pontano and Summonte. In the opening scenes Pontano welcomes the newcomers Suardino and Peto and relates Giles's sermon to the people; in the final scene he relates Giles's discourse to his friends, which encourages Suardino and Peto to return to the academy. These opening and closing scenes flank two discussions of predestination and human freedom. In the first discussion, Pontano denies the influence of nature in human visions and prophecies, and in the second, Pardo asserts the existence of free will against the physical determinism of astrology. Within these discussions are two pairs of erudite *quaestiones*. In the first half of the dialogue, Carbone poses a Virgilian problem for Pucci and Tamira; and Tomacelli asks Marchese and Caracciolo to compare the Elysian fields and the Christian paradise. In the second half of the dialogue, Chariteo delivers a grammatical exegesis of Hermetic doctrine, and Pardo supplements it with his own observations on grammar.

The central passage of the dialogue is an exchange between Pontano and Summonte concerning the deaths of Altilio and Calenzio and the voluntary exile of Sannazaro. The news of Calenzio's death represents the culmination of the personal losses of Pontano's circle—Compatre, Altilio, and Calenzio—giving the scene a symmetry which emphasizes its central position in the dialogue.[10] The heart of the exchange is Summonte's evocation of Sannazaro's departure and the recitation of his elegiac farewell to Naples. Summonte quotes the poem in order to provide a sort of recreation from the learned questions of the circle (p. 267: *recreamentum . . . quasi quoddam quaestionum haud multo ante explicatarum*). The verses evoke the various themes of *Aegidius*—farewell, Muses and Sirens, garden pleasures—and Summonte's description of Sannazaro's noble departure recalls Ferrando Gennaro's oracular promise in the dialogue *Actius* to return to his friends.[11] This scene is the ideal center of the dialogue, representing a respite from laborious grammatical discussions in the affectionate fellowship of the academy. The commemorative nature of *Aegidius* is here dramatically symbolized in the combination of poetic beauty (Sannazaro's lyric) and personal longing (*desiderium*). The desire for learned companionship, from which the humanist dialogue sprang in Bruni's *Dialogus I*, assumes here a transcendent significance: the memory of Sannazaro survives just as the piety of Altilio and Calenzio survives in the affectionate memory of the academy.[12]

After this central scene, Chariteo expounds the word of God (*verbum Dei*), according to Hermetic doctrine, as the source of creation. His exposition is a fitting introduction to the second half of *Aegidius*, in which verbal and grammatical discussions predominate, for Chariteo exalts the notion of the Word as the primary source of being and divinity. His apotheosis of grammar, the study of words, anticipates the verbal distinctions of both Pardo and Giles in the second half of the dialogue, and lends them an importance which must not be overlooked. Preaching before the people, Giles had synthesized various aspects of Christ's divinity (p. 249: "Christ, then, is the good, the truth, and the light, and He is the life"). Speaking to a small gathering of humanists in a monastery garden, Giles analyzes the distinctions between the Latin equivalents for Aristotle's Greek vocabulary. The private and academic nature of Giles's grammatical discourse is a necessary complement to the piety and good works of his public preaching, as Suardino implies at the end of the dialogue when he observes that Giles is restoring the Augustinian order to its former mastery of ancient eloquence.

The unity of *Aegidius* is created not only by these larger structural symmetries but also by recurrent images and themes. Allusions to the Muses and to gardens pervade the work. In the opening scene when Pontano welcomes Suardino and Peto to his home, he offers them the "gifts of the Muses," whom he identifies with Christ (p. 247). Citing Virgil, Pontano attributes to the Muses the omniscience of natural events, and his allusion to them elicits Suardino's recollection of Mariano, the friar who cultivated the "Christian Muses" (p. 249). We may be consoled, Pontano observes, for the Christian Muses have elected Giles to succeed Mariano; and after recounting Giles's sermon, Pontano adds that it was inspired by Mariano "through the Christian Muses" (p. 252). The religious oracle of Altilio counsels the academy to cultivate the Christian Muses, who are piety and religion, and to dedicate their gift of expression (*oratio*) to Christ, not to idle recreations. Later, when Pontano recalls the exile of Sannazaro, his grief is mitigated because the steadfast virtue of the poet has vouchsafed him the escort of the Muses, who are the symbol of Sannazaro's devotion to Naples and her king.

Associated with the Muses are the garden nymphs of Pontano's rural estates; and in the outdoor gathering of *Aegidius*, a dialogue permeated by the spirit of Virgil's *Georgics* and by their appeal to nature's teachings, the evocation of garden settings assumes a symbolic importance peculiar to its philosophical and religious themes. Recalling Book III of Valla's *De vero falsoque bono*, Caracciolo's explication of the word *paradise* (Greek for "garden") combines the notion of pleasure with that of the enjoyment (*fruitio*) of man's highest good, divine illumination.[13] In bidding farewell to Naples, Sannazaro's poem salutes the rustic leisure of academic gatherings as well as Pontano's learned poetry ("Hesperides," p. 262). Finally, it is in a garden setting at the monastery of San Giovanni a Carbonara that Giles offers philological observations to his friends Pontano, Carbone, and Chariteo during the walk that Pontano describes at the end of the dialogue. As in Erasmus' later colloquy *Convivium religiosum*, the garden serves as an ideal site for pious discussion, and Giles appropriately cites Virgil's *Georgics* (IV, 418) in his discourse (p. 281).[14]

In addition to these thematic threads which unite the fabric of the discussion, there are recurring notes of sentiment and affection that unify the dialogue. In the first half of the dialogue, the longing (*desiderium*) of the interlocutors for the lamented Mariano, the exiled Sannazaro, and the departed Calenzio adds an emotional dimension to the figure of the aged Pontano, "remnant of an early age" (p. 245). But the commemorative retrospection of the initial discussion is gradually supplanted by assertions of optimism for the future. The complaints of Pucci and Pontano against the injustices of time (*iniquitas temporum*) are answered by more confident voices expressing the hope (*spes*) that a new and elegant Latin philosophy will soon emerge.

In the final scene of *Aegidius*, Pontano prefaces his account of Giles's conversation with his own ideal of the new Latin philosophy: "Although I am old and weighed down with age, I am yet possessed of the hope that before I leave you, I may see our Latin philosophy expounding its topics with a more refined style and elegance, and that abandoning this contentious manner of debating (*relicta hac litigiosa disputandi ratione*) it may adopt a more tranquil form of speech and discussion, using its own proper and purely Roman vocabulary" (p. 280). Pontano's ideal is not a mere stylistic program fostered by the academy's refinement. Following the tradition of the humanist dialogue, particularly the example of Valla, Pontano insists that philosophy presupposes the study and emendation of language. The ideal philosophy adumbrated in Pontano's dialogues is necessarily a Latin philosophy which requires extensive grammatical investigation and scrupulous verbal distinctions.

The basis of the new Latin philosophy—that is, of the Latin language—is for Pontano, as for Valla, usage.[15] The notion of usage is twofold, practical and linguistic. The practical meaning of usage corresponds to the *usus communis* of Poggio and Valla, providing an important touchstone for testing the validity of human truths. The linguistic sense of usage is more restricted, but even in the academic setting of *Aegidius* it does not imply a rigorous classicism. Indeed, Pardo's discussion of the Latin words *privatio* and *carentia* concludes that the former is sanctioned by centuries of usage, despite Cicero's authoritative endorsement of the latter.

Discussing the immortality of the soul, Pontano early in the dialogue formulates the historical theory implicit in his linguistic and philosophical ideal of pristine Latinity. He appeals to the universality and antiquity of the popular belief in the soul's immortality as proof of the natural truth of the notion. This holy and ancient belief, he argues, grew up with man from the beginning of the world, just as religion is planted in man by nature. And just as the popular belief in the soul's immortality is ancient and natural (p. 253: *antiquissima . . . ac naturalis*), so the consequent popular practice of funeral rites is ancient and in strict accordance with nature (p. 254: *antiquissimum . . . maximeque secundum naturam*). From the universal observance of piety toward the dead, Pontano derives the universal truth of the soul's immortality, adducing the clear consensus of all nations (p. 254: *manifestissimus gentium quidem omnium consensus*) as compelling evidence of that truth.

The antiquity of this belief confirms its accordance with nature, Pontano observes, for it is shared by those closest to mankind's origin (p. 254: *qui rerum origini propiores fuere*), the founders of society and human institutions. Yet the initial harmony of man and nature—apparent in Pontano's four-year-old son, who senses the immanence of God in nature—has been recently destroyed, Pontano laments, by petty philosophers and ignorant scientists who have revived the false notion of the soul's dissolution at death. Both depraved and impious, this recent opinion originated not among the people but among profligate men of learning. Like those who misused the sword, ax, and knife, which were invented for man's daily needs, by employing them in quarrels and murders, so the modern *litterati* have misused their talents and their learning in promulgating this impious doctrine.

The separation of learning (*litterae*) from man's natural beliefs and from the practical realities of human life is the source of pernicious impiety. Pontano looks to an earlier age for the unspoiled propriety of a language in harmony with man and nature. He finds this harmony in the pristine setting of rural life and in the simple elegance of agricultural language in Virgil's *Georgics*. After the academy has heard Altilio's oracle exhorting them to Christian piety, Carbone poses a problem concerning the poetics of Virgil's *Georgics*. Because his proposal seems abrupt, Tomacelli later feels obliged to excuse Carbone's apparent lapse from piety by observing that ancient poets often anticipated Christian teachings in their verse. But in fact Carbone's digression occasions a significant remark from Pucci on the pristine state of Italian agriculture, which points the same moral as Pontano's earlier animadversions on recent philosophers. In Virgil's day, Pucci explains, farmers in Latium, as in all of Italy, were so aware of the importance of the agricultural site that Virgil could omit general observations about the desirable qualities of a field and could begin at once with precepts for the sowing of crops. In the preceding scene of the dialogue, Pontano notes the modern decline of both philosophy and agriculture, observing that the farmers of the day too often neglect the importance of the site and climate of their fields, just as philosophers overlook man's divine nature.

A subsequent reference to Virgil's *Georgics* in *Aegidius* reveals a similar appeal to the practical basis of language by demonstrating the importance of the natural experiences of agriculture in the development of Pontano's Latin philosophy. In the conversation in the monastery gardens, Giles discusses the Latin word *dispositio,* which the medieval translators of Aristotle had used to render the Greek *diathesis*. Their usage is improper, Giles explains, tracing the original meaning of the word to its agricultural sense of aligning vines and trees, as in Virgil's *Eclogues* (I, 73). Since the Greek word does not correspond in sense to the original or subsequent usage of *dispositio,* Giles proposes the noun *habilitas* as the correct translation of *diathesis,* citing the meaning of "innate or natural suitability" which the adjective *habilis* connotes in Virgil's *Georgics* (IV, 418).[16] Correct usage is that which is closest to the ancient origins of language during the age of man's pristine harmony with nature.

The propriety of language is thus defined by its concrete significance in denoting practical realities, and even the higher planes of Pontano's Latin philosophy will not lose contact with the realm of concrete reality. Valla had established the concrete notion of pleasure as a basis for the higher notion of celestial beatitude. Caracciolo prefaces his discussion of paradise in *Aegidius* with the observation that we must treat divine matters with the same words employed in talking and reasoning about human affairs (p. 265: *nec nos de Deo cum disserimus aliis quidem verbis quam cum de homine et loquimur et disputamus*). The language of his discussion recalls the concrete expression of Valla's Antonio da Rho, and this concrete quality is the more striking for Marchese's promise that Caracciolo is to discuss Christian paradise "in Christian language" (p. 265: *Christiano sermone*).

The inspiration for the Christian language of the academy must presumably come, as Pontano's comment on the sermon of Giles suggests, from the Christian Muses of Altilio's oracular injunction. It is characteristic of Pontano's syncretic vision in *Aegidius,* revealed in the verbal and thematic unities of the dialogue, that the oracle of

Altilio is itself couched in the concrete language of agriculture. The playful *juvenilia* composed by academy members "in the flower of their youth," Altilio's apparition warns, must now be abandoned since the academy has matured and, like flowers past their bloom, ought to bring forth fruits worthy of man's divine nature (p. 256). The oracle is welcomed by Pontano, who resumes the agricultural metaphor to exhort his fellow academicians to reap the fruits worthy of their maturity. Agriculture becomes a symbol for the harmonious role of man in nature, uniting the academy's "cultivation" of the Muses with the natural piety and religion "implanted" (p. 253: *insita*) in man's soul by God.

As in Pontano's other dialogues, the method of *Aegidius* is synthetic, not analytic. Instead of the two- or three-part debate of earlier humanist dialogues, there is a gradual accretion of learning advanced in observance of the academy rule that all present must speak (p. 260: *disserendi locus suus . . . cuique relinquendus*); and there is a cumulative sense of individual contributions unified by Pontano's creative vision. The rule of the academy originated with the custom of its founder, Antonio Beccadelli, who was accustomed to pose questions or to expound on subjects (*Antonius,* p. 54). In *Aegidius,* Carbone and Tomacelli propound questions for others, but on the whole the dialogue consists of discourses volunteered by the interlocutors. Pontano's ideal of the Latin philosophy of the future insists that contentious debate yield to tranquil discussion.

Like other humanist dialogues, Pontano's dialogues depict the leisurely discussions of eclectic philosophers for whom discussion constitutes an intellectual exercise complementary to other activities, not a profession excluding variety and informality. The lengthy disquisitions of *Actius,* for example, require the diversion provided by lesser grammatical questions, and the recitation of poetry in *Antonius* and *Aegidius* provides interludes of tranquil diversion that are needed to offset the serious tone of the discussion. This need for recreation among eclectic philosophers recalls the paradigm of Cicero's *De oratore,* in which the excursus of Caesar on wit in Book II provides a humorous refreshment from the technical expositions of the main discussion on the orator.

The eclectic philosophers of the academy, besides requiring variety within their own discussions, caution repeatedly against the proclivity of professional philosophers who, in a blind devotion to theory, lose sight of practical realities and human obligations. This attitude of common sense and moderation is most clearly expressed in Pontano's first dialogue, *Charon,* in which the underworld ferryman of the title appears as an amateur philosopher always conscious of his practical duties. For Charon, philosophical discussion is a pursuit for "leisure hours" (p. 8: *succisiva tempora*).[17] 'Philosophy is for him literally an "avocation" liable to call us away from our active duties (p. 17: *videndum . . .ne nostrum hoc quaerendi studium ab agendis nos re&us avocet;* p. 28: *nec committendum ut, dum sciendi voluptate capimur, ab agendis rebus . . . avocemur*).

By the same token, the discussions of the academy constantly warn against vain speculations and strive to maintain close contact with the outside world (*Charon*, p. 17; *Antonius*, p. 93). Exchanges with passersby and the reports of academy travelers in *Charon* and *Antonius* provide material for satirical comment in a Lucianic vein, while the placid gathering of *Aegidius* compares itself favorably with the Florentine and Roman academies recently visited by Pucci and Tamira. Accounts of the world beyond the academy, such as Suppazio's *iter Neapolitanum* related in *Antonius*, serve to sketch the historical actualities which form the background of the discussion and occasionally influence it. Suppazio, for instance, concludes from his journey that notions of "right and wrong are determined more by local usage than by natural principles" (p. 93: *probum improbumque pro locis, populis, nationibus iudicari, neque tam naturam quam leges atque instituta sequi aliaque alibi laudari*). The historical relativism of Poggio's dialogues is based on the same sort of contemporary reportage.[18]

Pontano's dialogues have much in common with those of Poggio, and readers as early as Erasmus could not mistake the affinity of the two authors' anticlerical polemics.[19] For both Poggio and Pontano, moreover, the dialogue provides a convenient form in which to discuss topics either entirely new or inadequately treated by ancient authors. Pontano's *Actius*, a dialogue on "poetic meters and the art of writing history," purports—like Poggio's dialogues—to provide a foundation for further discussion of its subject. In *Actius*, Sannazaro's first discourse on metrics ends with a passage reminiscent of Poggio: "Perhaps I took too long and was too ambitious in explaining these matters, but I did so the more willingly because no one to my knowledge has written about this. Although I pased over many points, others will analyze them more keenly and explain them more suitably" (p. 161). This sense of progress in knowledge envisions the participation of both interlocutors and readers, and it asserts the freedom of both. Discussing Virgilian textual variants in *Actius*, Sannazaro explains his own reading but then concludes, "while such is my opinion, let each judge for himself" (p. 155: *de hoc sit suum cuiusque iudicium, nostra quidem haec est opinio*).

Altilio's commentary on historiography in *Actius* shares this sense of tentative novelty in discussing a subject previously neglected. When Puderico first requests Altilio's treatment of history, he notes the lack of theoretical writings on the subject:

> I am greatly moved by a burning desire to hear something about history, which has had no expounders, while grammar, rhetoric, and philosophy have found many instructors, great and excellent at that. Although I know that there are many things to be said on the subject that cannot be discussed in one fortuitous gathering, yet I wish to entreat and persuade Altilio to succeed Sannazaro in order of speaking and to discourse more elaborately on this subject—or at least to suggest the main points, as they say, so that we may hear something from him, whether an exposition or an outline of history. (p. 192)

When Altilio accepts the task of discussing history, he confirms Puderico's assertion that the topic has had no classical exponent and agrees simply to suggest (*innuere*) the main points rather than to provide a systematic treatment (*praecipere*).[20] The dialogue thus provides a less rigid format for dealing with a new subject. Like Alberti's *Libri della Famiglia*, *Actius* presents a modern and relevant compilation of diverse sources. Puderico hails Altilio's discussion of historiography as the first step on the way to a systematic ordering of that science, implicitly inviting Pontano's readers to continue the discussion in their own work: "We all confess, Altilio, that you have equaled your promises and afforded us immense pleasure by your discussion, having collected this dispersed and widely scattered material and then assembled it in proper order, so that those who may later wish to reduce it to a system (*praecepta*) will have an easy task."[21] Similarly, in treating Carbone's Virgilian question in *Aegidius*, Pucci observes that no grammarians have yet proposed a solution (p. 261: *ratio illa nondum a grammaticis prodita est*). Caracciolo also prefaces his remarks on paradise by indicating that he can only suggest the main points.

Grammar (*grammatica*) has unusual importance in Pontano's dialogues, with their lengthy disquisitions on grammatical problems. For Pontano, as for Valla, the basis of philosophy is language. Valla provides the philosophical complement to his dialogues in his treatises on language and logic, *Elegantiae* and *Dialecticae disputationes*, and Pontano includes numerous grammatical investigations in his dialogues, having composed the treatises *De sermone* and *De aspiratione* and well.[22]

The classical definition of *grammatica* was formulated by Seneca in one of his '*Moral Epistles* (88, 3): "Grammar is concerned with attention to language: if allowed wider scope, with histories: if extended to its furthest limits, with poetry." The academic discussions of Pontano's dialogues treat exactly such problems, and *Actius*, a dialogue on poetry and history, merits the title of the greatest grammatical dialogue of the Quattrocento.[23] *Antonius* as well is concerned largely with grammatical questions, and its polemics against the ancient grammarians Macrobius and Gellius disguise an attack on the modern *arbiter Elegantiarum* Valla, the great grammarian who had called in question the supremacy of Cicero. The observation of Caracciolo in *Aegidius* to the effect that, in discussing divine matters, one must use the language of human affairs shows that the grammatical concerns of Pontano's dialogues are not merely the pastimes or polemics they may seem to be but also constitute a necessary foundation for discussing the higher problems of what Pontano significantly calls a Latin philosophy. Like Valla, Pontano insists on the primacy of verbal investigations as the basis for examining ethical and natural questions.

Like earlier humanist dialogues, Pontano's dialogues establish a polarity between the inner group of the learned gathering and the outer society of the contemporary world. In Pontano's first dialogue, *Charon*, the mythological settilng allows vivid satirical evocations of Italian events and persons, while the learned discussions of the underworld only indirectly reflect the academy at Naples—with the exception of a single playful reference to Beccadelli and Pontano, whom a defunct grammarian wishes to correct on points of Latin usage (p. 36).[24] In later dialogues, numerous details refer to the author's own experience. The autobiographical allusiveness of Pontano's dialogues is one of their characteristic features; and although Pontano himself appears as an interlocutor in only two of his dialogues, *Asinus* and *Aegidius*, all of them are in a sense autobiographical documents, which evoke their author's personality more than do the humanist dialogues of the early Quattrocento.[25] Charon, the Lyrist in *Antonius*, and Sannazaro in *Actius*—all present the poet-author wearing a different mask. In *Asinus*, Pontano appears as the protagonist of an allegorical comedy, returning from his diplomatic tasks in Rome to private life in Naples. In *Aegidius*, Pontano appears in the magisterial role of the erudite and pious leader of the academy, a model of ancient virtue (p. 245: *prisci reliquiae temporis*) and a modern Socrates who calmly awaits death in the assurance of leaving a significant moral legacy.[26]

The idealized portrait of the academy in Pontano's dialogues depicts the practical realization of true intellectual, moral, and religious virtues which are repeatedly contrasted to the false views and values of the world. Within the academy, grammatical erudition is the basis of refined composition and of the new Latin philosophy. In the outside world, pedantic fury inspires the rampages of violent grammarians, the rabid whelps of *Antonius.*[27] Within the academy, the ideal of wisdom (*sapientia*) combines learning with piety, and virtue, the link between God and man, comprises right deeds and noble words. In the outside world, the vain disputes of theologians and the profligate lives of clerics demonstrate the madness (*delirium*) caused by the separation of philosophy and morality.[28] Within the academy, finally, true religion means an understanding of man's relation to God and nature. In the outside world, corrupt teachers promulgate vicious and impious doctrines, while the populace suffers from superstitious beliefs and practices fostered by a self-seeking clergy.[29]

As in Poggio's dialogues, the overt polemics of Pontano's *Charon* and *Antonius* are conducted within acknowledged limits. When Aeacus, in *Charon,* asks Mercury to discuss the qualities of Italian rulers, he is told that the topic is "unsafe to discuss in the upper world and unnecessary in the lower" (p. 23: *et illic apud mortales de iis loqui satis tutum non est et hic apud vos parum . . . necessarium*). Deploring the decline of public morality in Naples, Pietro Compatre, in *Antonius,* likewise observes that "since we may accuse rather than remedy the situation, and since it is unsafe, let us stop discussing the morals of the populace" (p. 51: *quando accusari haec possunt magis quam corrigi nec satis est tutum, dicere de populi moribus desinamus*).

Pontano continues Poggio's antiecclesiastical satire, in *Charon* especially, where generally mordant comments are elaborated in anticlerical tales and supplemented by mention of specific individuals. In the initial scenes of *Antonius* and *Actius,* Pontano's interlocutors lament the present decline of clerical morality and cite Cicero's celebrated exclamation "o tempora, o mores" (pp. 56, 131). Suppazio in *Antonius* testifies to the widespread association of friars and theologians with prostitutes.

The greatest decline lamented in Pontano's dialogues is the decline of philosophy, a Petrarchan theme prominent in humanist dialogues. The faulty and ignorant translation and interpretation of Aristotle by medieval and Scholastic philosophers and theologians arouse the humanist indignation of interlocutors in both *Charon* and *Aegidius,* thereby linking Pontano's first and last dialogues. In *Charon,* the current state of Aristotelian studies occasions important reflections on the history of philosophical thought. Recalling his own conversation with Aristotle in the underworld, Charon marvels at how difficult an author Aristotle continues to be after so many centuries—an observation which recalls that of Niccoli in Bruni's *Dialogus I.* Mercury in turn relates the caustic witticisms which a clever orator (p. 15: *rhetor,* suggesting Valla) directed against a philosopher-theologian for distorting the sense of Aristotelian texts. When Charon responds that Aristotle's obscurity might excuse the theologian, Mercury protests: "Obscurity by no means accounts for everything. Rather, it seems to me that there are two reasons for this state of affairs. First, those who practice philosophy today are ignorant of fine literature, to which Aristotle himself made a considerable contribution. Second, dialectic has been corrupted, first by the Germans and the French, and then by Italians as well, and it is in dialectic that the philosophers still wreak the greatest havoc" (p. 15).

In *Aegidius,* the medieval translators of Aristotle are twice impugned, and it is a source of hope to the academy that new translations are being undertaken (p. 260). In a speech patterned on that of Bruni's Niccoli, Pucci traces the decline of eloquence:

> The injustices of the times caused eloquence to be separated from the study of the sciences for many centuries, whereas no one before had been learned without being eloquent as well. But the pursuit of eloquence died out completely after the fall of the Roman Empire, and hardly a trace of grammar itself remained. The sciences, on the contrary, were cultivated in great honor, as is clearly shown by the host of natural scientists and theologians which arose after Boethius, in Spain and in France, in England and even in Germany.[30]

But Pucci adds that Pontano is now reuniting science and eloquence, and that his exhortations and example serve to arouse (*incendere*) others to the pursuit of eloquence.[31]

The magisterial figure of the aged Pontano arousing a younger generation of scholars to productive endeavors calls to mind the similar role of Salutati in Bruni's *Dialogus I* a century earlier; and the concerns of the two, despite differences in setting, reveal the striking continuity of themes in the Quattrocento humanist dialogue. In both Bruni and Pontano, discussion provides a social stimulus for the pursuit of eloquence and the revival of classical studies. Both writers portray the dramatic continuity of learning between old and new generations. In Pontano's *Aegidius,* the circle of the academy is open to visitors who may disseminate the humanist learning of Naples, and the dialogue ends significantly with the promise of Suardino and Peto to attend the academy daily during their stay in Naples (p. 284: *quotidianasque istas consessiones assidui frequentabimus*).

The circle of Salutati in Florence is nevertheless far removed from the Neapolitan Academy under Pontano. The secular and local continuities established by Bruni's *Dialogi* bear a closer resemblance to the spirit of Alberti's *Libri della Famiglia*, whereas Pontano's *Aegidius* follows the tradition of Poggio and Valla when it offers a religious synthesis of classical and Christian elements—achieved peacefully, not polemically, as a harmonious reconciliation of Aristotelian doctrine and Augustinian piety in the figure of Giles. Although the aim of both Bruni and Pontano is to achieve a final consensus in their dialogues, their diverse methods reflect the differences of climate between the militant humanism of the first half of the century and the academic syncretism of the second. The vivid Florentine background of Bruni's *Dialogi* presents the bright dawn of the humanist dialogue in the clash of personalities and arguments, while the softened glow of pious discourse in Pontano's *Aegidius* calls to mind Longinus' characterization in *On the Sublime* of Homer's *Odyssey* as a work of the author's discursive old age, to be likened to the setting sun, having grandeur without intensity (9, 13). In Pontano's ideal of placid discussion, the spirit of controversy of the early Quattrocento yields to the discursive classicism of the Cinquecento. The last echoes of the rigorous and polemical debates of humanism fade, to be supplanted by the refined accents of courtly gatherings in the *volgare* dialogue.

Notes
Index

Notes

I. Cicero and the Humanist Dialogue

Epigraph: Francesco Petrarca, *Prose,* ed. G. Martellotti, P. G. Ricci, E. Carrara, E. Bianchi, La letteratura italiana, Storia e testi, 7 (Milan-Naples: Ricciardi, 1955), p. 134: "suam quisque sententiam sequatur; est enim, ut nosti, opinionum ingens varietas libertasque iudicandi." All citations for Petrarch's *Secretum* refer to this edition.

1. Rudolf Hirzel, *Der Dialog: Ein literar-historischer Versuch* (1895; rpt., Hildesheim: Georg Olms, 1963), I, 68-83.

2. Hirzel, *Der Dialog,* I, 457-550; Ernst Becker, *Technik and Szenerie des ciceronischen Dialogs* (Osnabrück: Obermeyer, 1938).

3. Cf. Eckhard Kessler, "Autobiographie als philosophisches Argument? Ein Aspekt des Philosophierens bei Cicero und die gegenwärtige Praxis des Philosophs," in *Studia Humanitatis: Ernesto Grassi zum 70. Geburtstage,* ed. Eginhard Hora and Eckhard Kessler, Humanistische Bibliothek, I, 16 (Munich: Wilhelm Fink, 1973), pp. 173-187.

4. Hirzel, *Der Dialog,* I, 376-379; Henri-Irénée Marrou, *Saint Augustin et la fin de la culture antique* (Paris: De Boccard, 1938).

5. Giovanna Wyss Morigi, *Contributo allo studio del dialogo all'epoca dell'Umanesimo e del Rinascimento* (Monza, 1947); Francesco Tateo, *Tradizione e realtà nell'Umanesimo italiano* (Bari: Dedalo, 1967), pp. 221-421. On the Curia, see Lapo da Castiglionchio, *Dialogus de curiae commodis,* ed. Richard Scholz, "Eine humanistische Schilderung der Kurie aus dem Jahre 1438," *Quellen und Forschungen aus italienischen Archiven und Bibliotheken,* XVI, i (1913), 108-163; Enea Silvio Piccolomini, *Tractatus,*

ed. G. Cugnoni, *Atti dell'Accademia dei Lincei,* ser. III, fasc. VIII (1882-1883), 555; W. von Hofmann, *Forschungen zur Geschichte der Kurialen Behörden vom Schisma bis zur Reformation,* Bibliothek des kgl. preussischen historischen Instituts in Rom, XII-XII (1913; rpt., Turin: Bottega d'Erasmo, 1971), esp. I, 147-152; II, 105-114.

6. Platina (Bartolomeo Sacchi), *De optimo cive, De falso et vero bono, Contra amores, De vera nobilitate,* in *Opera* (Venice, 1511); Giovannantonio Campano, *De ingratitudine fugienda,* in *Opera* (Venice, 1502); Cristoforo Landino, *De anima,* ed. A. Paoli and G. Gentile, *Annali di Università Toscane,* 34 (1915), 1-50; 35 (1916), 1-138; 36 (1917), 1-96; Landino, *De vera nobilitate,* ed. Maria Teresa Liaci, Nuova collezione di testi umanistici inediti o rari, 15 (Florence: Olschki, 1970); Landino, *Disputationes camuldulenses* (Florence, 1480).

7. See Hirzel, *Der Dialog,* I, 174-268.

8. Leon Battista Alberti, *Pontifex,* in *Opera inedita et pauca separatim impressa,* ed. Girolamo Mancini (Florence: Sansoni, 1890); Lorenzo Valla, *De libero arbitrio, De professione religiosorum,* in *Prosatori latini del Quattrocento,* ed. E. Garin, La letteratura italiana, Storia e testi, 13 (Milan-Naples: Ricciardi, 1952).

9. Hirzel, *Der Dialog,* I, 151-160; II, 137-138, 259-261, 352-358; Josef Martin, *Symposion: Geschichte einer literarischen Form* (Paderborn: F. Schöningh, 1931).

10. Francesco Filelfo, *Convivia mediolanensia* (Milan, 1477); Angelo Decembrio, *Politia litteraria* (Augsburg, 1540).

11. Hirzel, *Der Dialog,* II, 269-333.

12. Leon Battista Alberti, *Intercoenales,* in *Opera inedita* and in E. Garin, "Venticinque Intercenali inedite," *Rinascimento,* II, 4 (1964), 125-258; Alberti, *Momus o del Principe,* ed. Giuseppe Martini, Scrittori politici italiani, 13 (Bologna: Zanichelli, 1942); Maffeo Vegio, *Philalethes* and *De felicitate et miseria,* in *Opera* (Lodi, 1613).

13. Pandolfo Collenuccio, *Opere volgari,* ed. A. Saviotti (Bari: Laterza, 1929); Antonio Galateo, *Eremita,* in *Prosatori latini del Quattrocento,* pp. 1068-1125; Giovanni Pontano, *Dialoghi,* ed. C. Previtera (Florence: Sansoni, 1943)..

14. Erasmus, *Opus epistolarum,* ed. P. S. Allen, II (Oxford: Oxford University Press, 1910), 99; see also *The Correspondence of Erasmus,* trans. R. A. B. Mynors and D. F. S. Thomson, III (Toronto-Buffalo: University of Toronto Press, 1976), 122. Although Erasmus' allusion to Poggio is generally taken to refer to the *Facetiae,* the antiecclesiastical satire of his dialogues ("impia") may also be meant.

15. For Petrarch's *Secretum,* see Francisco Rico, *Vida u obra de Petrarca: I. Lectura del "Secretum"* (Padua: Editrice Antenore, 1974); Adelia Noferi, *L'esperienza poetica del Petrarca* (Florence: Sansoni, 1962), pp. 236-284; Francesco Tateo, *Dialogo interiore e polemica ideologica nel "Secretum" del Petrarca* (Florence: Sansoni, 1965), pp. 15-19; Remigio Sabbadini, "Note filologiche sul 'Secretum del Petrarca," *Rivista di filologia e d'istruzione*

classica, 45 (1919), 24-37; Hans Baron, *From Petrarch to Leonardo Bruni: Studies in Humanistic and Political Literature* (Chicago-London: University of Chicago Press, 1968), pp. 51-101.

16. In the *Secretum*, as in the salutations of his letters to men of classical antiquity (*Familiares*, XXIV), Petrarch employs his Christian name, "Franciscus," to represent his modern self in dialogue with figures of the past.

17. See Walter Rüegg, *Cicero und der Humanismus: Formale Untersuchungen über Petrarca und Erasmus* (Winterthur, 1946), pp. 46-48.

18. Rico, *Lectura del "Secretum,"* p. 34n99.

19. See Petrarch, *Fam.*, XXI, 12, 27; XXIV, 5, 2.

20. For this device, see Cicero, *De amicitia*, 1, 3; Plato, *Theaetetus* (143c); Sabbadini, "Note filologiche," p. 29; Wyss Morigi, *Contributo*, p. 35; Rico, *Lectura del "Secretum,"* p. 35. See also Valla, *De libero arbitrio*; Machiavelli, *Dialogo intorno alla nostra lingua* and *Libri dell'arte della guerra*.

21. Petrarch similarly blushes in writing to his brother (*Fam.*, X, 5, 4) about their diverse spiritual progress, citing Augustine's *Confessions*.

22. Cf. Augustinus, p. 32: "unum illud indignor, quod fieri quenquam vel esse miserum suspicaris invitum"; Cicero, *Tusculanae disputationes*, V, 5, 12: "Non mihi videtur ad beate vivendum satis posse virtutem." See also Rico, *Lectura*, pp. 45, 64.

23. See Rüegg, *Cicero*, p. 49.

24. See Cicero, *Tusc. disp.*, I, 21, 49; Noferi, *L'esperienza poetica*, p. 253n1.

25. Cf. Martin Grabmann, *Die Geschichte der Scholastischen Methode* (1909-1911: rpt. Darmstadt: Wissenschaftliche Buchgesellschaft, 1957), I, 130, 140.

26. See Noferi, *L'esperienza poetica*, p. 252. The phrase *experientia magistra* recurs in Petrarch, *Fam.*, XII, 12, 4; XIV, 1, 22; XIX, 3, 20; XXIII, 12, 8.

27. Cf. Augustine, *Confessions*, VII, 7, 17. Earlier in the *Secretum* (p. 36), Augustinus' magisterial "expertus loquor" contrasts with Franciscus' "tristis experior."

28. In fact, Petrarch describes *De vera religione* as a celebrated foreign city which he had entered for the first time (p. 66), an image recalling his list of favorite books and its Senecan motto. See B. L. Ullman, *Studies in the Italian Renaissance* (Rome: Edizioni di storia e letteratura, 1955), pp. 117-137.

29. Augustinus cites a verse of Publilius. See Rico, *Lectura*, p. 77n85. The endorsement by Augustinus of moderate contention reverses the historical Augustine's approval of soliloquy.

30. See Rico, *Lectura*, p. 270.

II. Leonardo Bruni and the Origin of Humanist Dialogue

Epigraph: Leonardo Bruni, in *Prosatori latini del Quattrocento*, pp. 46-48: "quid est, per deos immortales, quod ad res subtiles cognoscendas atque discutiendas plus valere possit quam disputatio, ubi rem in medio positam velut oculi plures undique speculantur, ut in ea nihil sit quod subterfugere, nihil quod latere, nihil quod valeat omnium frustrari intuitum?" All citations from Bruni's *Dialogi ad Petrum Histrum* refer to this edition.

1. See esp. Hans Baron, *The Crisis of the Early Italian Renaissance* (Princeton: Princeton University Press, 1955—hereafter referred to as Crisis[1]); rev. ed. (1966—hereafter referred to as *Crisis*[2]).

2. Cf. Baron, *Crisis*[1], I, 201-203. See also R. Sabbadini, review of E. De Franco, *I dialoghi al Vergerio*, in *Giornale storico della letteratura italiana*, 96 (1930), 129-133; Tateo, *Tradizione*, pp. 236-240.

3. See e.g. Bruni, *Epistulae*, ed. L. Mehus (Florence, 1741), II, 15; III, 19.

4. On the overcoming of distance by affection, see Seneca, *Epistulae morales*, 55, 9; Petrarch, *Fam.*, II, 6, 3; Bruni, *Humanistische-philosophische Schriften*, ed. H. Baron (Leipzig: Teubner, 1928), p. 139.

5. Baron, *Crisis*[1], I, 210-215.

6. P. 40 (Salutati): "Quid est quod ingenium magis acuat . . . quam disputatio? . . . Ut faciliter intelligi possit, hoc exercitatione excitatum ad cetera discernenda fieri velocius"; *Ep.*, I, 3 (to Salutati): "studia illa, atque exercitationes nostras, in quibus tu ceu ferro ferrum acuisse nos dicebas."

7. *De oratore*, I, 8, 30-34; *Dialogus I*, pp. 46-52. Cf. Crassus, *De or.*, I, 8, 34: "Quam ob rem pergite ut facitis, adulescentes, atque in id studium in quo estis incumbite, ut et vobis honori et amicis utilitati et rei publicae emolumento esse possitis"; Salutati, p. 52: "Quam ob rem vos obsecro, iuvenes, ut ad vestros laudabiles praeclarosque labores hanc unam, quae adhuc vos fugit, exercitationem addatis, ut utilitatibus undique comparatis facilius eo quo cupitis pervenire possitis."

8. Niccoli excepts Salutati as having a nearly divine genius, p. 60: "Tu mihi videris isto tuo praestantissimo ingenio ac paene divino, etiam his rebus deficientibus, sine quibus alii non possunt, haec assequi potuisse; itaque tu unus mihi sis ab hoc sermone exceptus." The passage imitates Crassus' praise of Antonius, who is likewise excepted for his divine genius, *De or.*, I, 38, 172: "Antoni incredibilis quaedam et prope singularis et divina vis ingenii videtur, etiam si hac scientia iuris nudata sit, posse se facile ceteris armis prudentiae tueri atque defendere, quam ob rem hic nobis sit exceptus."

9. For ineptitude in speaking, cf. Crassus *De or.*, I, 24, 111, and Niccoli's use of the notion to condemn ignorance (p. 52), the *dialectici* (p. 60), and Dante (p. 70). For impudence, cf. *De or.*, I, 101, 113, 128, 173, *and passim*, and Niccoli's condemnation of ignorance (p. 52), the *dialectici* (p. 58), and Petrarch (p. 72).

10. Sabbadini, review, p. 131, notes the resemblance between Niccoli's outburst (p. 68: "Quos tu mihi Dantes . . .?") and Scaevola's objection (*De or.*, I, 23, 105: "quem tu mihi . . . Staseam, quem Peripateticum narras?").

11. Crassus asks how great an orator would arise if endowed with both genius and the learning he himself lacks, *De or.*, I, 17, 79: "si tibi tantum in nobis videtur esse [sc. facultatis], quibus etiamsi ingenium, ut tu putas, non maxime defuit, doctrina certe et otium et hercule etiam studium illud discendi acerrimum defuit, quid censes, si ad alicuius ingenium vel maius illa, quae ego

non attigi, accesserint, qualem illum et quantum oratorem futurum?" Salutati (p. 64) asks what Niccoli might accomplish if he devoted himself to debating: "si is absque disputandi exercitatione, quae hoc maxime efficere potuit, tantum in respondendo valuit, quid putas illum, si ei rei operam dedisset, fuisse facturum?"

12. The closing formula—"Haec cum dixisset, surreximus"—echoes the end of Cicero's *De divinatione,* II, 72, 150. See Sabbadini, review.

13. Cf. Cicero, *De oratore,* ed. K. Kumaniecki (Leipzig: Teubner, 1969), pp. V-VIII.

14. Bruni's apparent imitation of passages in Cicero, *De or.*, I, 157-194, suggests his knowledge of this completer text. Yet the limits of such *Quellenforschung* are suggested by the affinities between passages of Bruni's *Dialogus I* and parts of *De oratore* I which were unknown in 1401. Cf. *De or.*, I, 47, 204: "sic ego intellego, si in haec, quae patefecit oratione sua Crassus, intrare volueritis, facillime vos ad ea quae cupitis, perventuros ab hoc aditu ianuaque patefacta," and *Dialogus I,* p. 60: "sunt . . . omnes viae addiscendi praeclusae, ut etiam si quis existat . . . discendi cupidus, tamen rerum difficultate impeditus, eo quo cupiat pervenire non possit."

15. Baron, *Crisis*[1], I, 201-203.

16. See Tateo, *Tradizione,* pp. 238, 243, 248-249.

17. Baron, *Crisis*[1], I, 202-203.

18. *De or.*, II, 10, 40: "tum Antonius 'heri enim' inquit 'hoc mihi proposueram ut si te refellissem, hos a te discipulos abducerem'"; *Dialogus II,* p. 96: "TUM NICOLAUS: 'Heri, inquit, mihi propositum erat ut libros tuos, Roberte, compararem; sciebam enim te si persuasissem, statim auctionem esse facturum.'"

19. Cf. the phrase "non repugnabo" in the recantations of Antonius (*De or.*, II, 8, 32) and Niccoli (*Dialogus II,* p. 82).

20. *De or.*, II, 7, 27: "'ego vero' inquit Crassus 'neque Antonium verbum facere patiar et ipse obmutescam, nisi prius a vobis impetraro'—'quidnam?' inquit Catulus—'ut hic sitis hodie'": *Dialogus II,* pp. 96-98: "'Ego vero, inquit ROBERTUS, non iubebo [sc. ut fores aperiantur] nisi prius mihi pollicearis . . . 'Quid' inquit COLUCIUS. 'Ut cras apud me omnes cenetis.'"

21. P. 94: "An vero illi extranei homines ita putabunt; nos autem cives in laude civis nostri erimus frigidiores? nec audebimus illum suis meritis ornare, praesertim cum hic vir studia humanitatis, quae iam extincta erant, repararit et nobis, quemadmodum discere possemus, viam aperuerit?" The passage echoes Bruni's Proem, where the humanities are described as "iam penitus extincta" (p. 44). See also Baron, *Crisis*[1], I, 231.

22. See Baron, *Crisis*[1], I, 231.

23. Boccaccio's promotion of Dante and Petrarch in Florence is succeeded by Niccoli's acts of devotion to all three poets in *Dialogus II,* p. 82.

24. Sabbadini, review.

25. Cf. *De or.*, I, 24, 111: "'Dicam equidem, quoniam institui, petamque a vobis,' inquit, 'ne has meas ineptias efferatis.'" Crassus' fear of seeming foolish reflects none of the fear of recrimination expressed by Niccoli, p. 70:

"Nunc Petrarcham consideremus, quamquam non me fugit, quam periculoso in loco verser, ut mihi sit etiam universi populi impetus pertimescendus, quem isti tui praeclari vates nugis nescio quibus . . . devinctum habent."

26. Cf. Baron, *Crisis*[1], I, 231-235.

27. Cf. Hirzel, *Der Dialog*, II, 378.

28. Cf. Baron, *Crisis*[2], pp. 113-118; Petrarch's *Secretum*, pp. 188-206.

29. Pp. 52-54: "Omnia sunt inter se mira quadam coniunctione annexa, nec pauca sine multis bene scire quisquam potest." Cf. *De or.*, III, 6, 21, and *De natura deorum*, I, 4, 9: "est enim admirabilis quaedam continuatio seriesque rerum, ut alia ex alia nexa et omnes inter se aptai conligataeque videantur."

30. Cicero, *Topica*, 1, 2-3. Describing the logical topics of disputation, Niccoli insists on a knowledge of "consequentium, antecedentium, causarum, effectum" (p. 52), a series perhaps derived from *Topica*, 23, 88: "loci autem convenient in eius generis quaestionem consequentis antecedentis repugnantis; adiuncti etiam eis qui sumuntur ex causis et effectis."

31., The questioning of Aristotle's authority is a Petrarchan theme. See e.g. Petrarch, *Fam.*, XX, 14, 9-12 (the "oracle" of Aristotle). On "Pythius Apollo," see Cicero, *Tusc. disp.*, I, 9, 17; Cicero, *Ad Brutum*, I, 2, 6 (cited in Petrarch, *Fam.*, XXII, 7, 23).

32. The Pythagorean preference for authority over reason is mentioned in Petrarch, *Fam.*, XXII, 3, 1, but without reference to discussion. Cicero's critique is resumed and elaborated in Lorenzo Valla, *Dialecticae disputationes*, *Opera omnia*, ed. Eugenio Garin (Turin: Bottega d'Erasmo, 1962), I, 643-645. Cf. Hirzel, *Der Dialog*, II, 379.

33. P. 68. Salutati repeats the phrase (p. 74). Niccoli objects to the "iudicium omnium" (p. 72). On Petrarch's popularity at Milan with even the *vulgus*, see *Fam.*, XIX, 16, 15. Where Niccoli specifies the "lanarii, pistores, atque eiusmodi turba" of the Florentine masses (p. 70), Petrarch had referred to the "fullones, textoresque et fabros in populo Arni" (*Fam.*, XXIV, 12, 37).

34. Salutati says that Bruni exaggerated Caesar's tyranny for rhetorical purposes, but he himself confesses a greater moral admiration for the republican figures Marcellus and Camillus (p. 78). Cf. *Crisis*[1], I, 215.

35. Christian Bec, *Les marchands écrivains: Affaires et humanisme à Florence, 1375-1434* (Paris-The Hague: Mouton, 1967), pp. 409-411.

III. Poggio Bracciolini and the Moral Debate

Epigraph: Poggio Bracciolini, *Opera omnia*, ed. Riccardo Fubini (Turin: Bottega d'Erasmo, 1964-1969), I, 100: "scio te vereri, ut quis eorum de quibus recte sentis se existimet a te offensum, sed vera loqui unicuique licet." All citations for Poggio's work refer to this edition. The letters, from the edition of Tommaso Tonelli (Florence, 1832-1861) which appears in vol. III of the Fubini edition, are cited as "Ton."

1. See esp. Ernst Walser, *Poggius Florentinus, Leben und Werke* (Leipzig: Teubner, 1914); Francesco Tateo, "Poggio Bracciolini e la dialogistica del Quattrocento," *Pubblicazioni dell'Università di Bari, Annali*

della Facoltà di Lettere e Filologia, 7 (1961), 167-204; Tateo, *Tradizione* (Bari: Dedalo, 1967), pp. 223-277; Helene Harth, "Niccolò Niccoli als literarischer Zensor: Untersuchungen zur Textgeschichte von Poggios 'De avaritia,'" *Rinascimento*, II, 7 (1967), 29-53; Riccardo Fubini, "Intendimenti umanistici e riferimenti patristici dal Petrarca al Valla," *Giornale storico della letteratura italiana*, 151 (1974), 520-578.

2. Cf. Ton. I, 273, 280; *De avaritia*, I, 1: "Quod si cui forte aut planum nimis atque humile videbitur dicendi genus, aut non satis explicata ratio muneris suscepti, is intelligat primum me delectari ea eloquentia, in qua non maior existat intelligendi quam legendi labor."

3. Cf. Harth, "Niccolò Niccoli," p. 35.

4. Cf. Tateo, *Tradizione*, p. 257. Poggio originally left a blank for the name of the classical orator (here "someone": *quendam*) who praised Dionysius and blamed Plato, and he asked Niccoli to supply the name, which he had forgotten (Ton. I, 275). Poggio may have had in mind a passage from Quintilian, *Inst. orat.*, II, 17, 4, in which a certain Polycrates is said to have praised the tyrant Busiris and blamed Socrates. At the same time as *De avaritia* was being composed, Leon Battista Alberti misquoted the Quintilian passage. See Alberti, *De commodis litterarum atque incommodis*, ed. Laura Goggi Carotti, Nuova collezione di testi umanistici inediti o rari, 17 (Florence: Olschki, 1976), pp. 40-41.

5. Cf. *Dialogus I*, p. 44: "Nicolaus . . . et in dicendo est promptus, et in lacessendo acerrimus," and Poggio's description of Niccoli in a letter of 1447 to Pietro Tommasi, Ton., II, 334: "vir acer, ac promptus . . . ad lacessendum." See also Poggio, *De infelicitate principum*, I, 394.

6. Antonio says to the newly arrived Andreas, "Te vero praesente tacemus pudore commoti, ne fias nostrarum censor ineptiarum," and Bartolomeo, "Ea est . . . ratio ut taceamus, cum te videamus et virum doctrissimum et theologum" (I, 6). See also Fubini, "Intendimenti," p. 563; Harth, "Niccolò Niccoli," p. 45.

7. Patristic texts are hereafter cited from Migne, *Patrologia latina* (*PL*) and *Patrologia graeca* (*PG*).

8. Cf. Gellius, *Noctes Atticae*, X, 5; Isidorus, *Origines*, X, 9.

9. The argument is imitated by Valla, *De vero falsoque bono*, ed. M. De Panizza Lorch (Bari: Adriatica, 1971), p. 87.

10. Cf. Augustine, *De libero arbitrio*, III, 17, 48 (*PL*, 32, 1294).

11. Cf. Aristotle, *Politics*, I, 7; VII, 8. The argument of animal instinct for self-preservation is used by Valla to defend pleasure in *De vero falsoque bono*, p. 35: "nihil est generi animantium tam a natura tributum quam ut se, vitam corpusque tueatur declinetque ea que nocitura videantur. Nunc autem quid magis vitam conservat quam voluptas?"

12. Cf. Hans Baron, "Franciscan Poverty and Civic Wealth," *Speculum*, 13 (1938), 31-33.

13. Cf. Petrarch, *Fam.*, XXIII, 12, 6: "omittamus ista magnifica et loquamur ut ceteri."

14. Cf. Chrysostom, *Sermon on John*, 65, 3 (*PG*, 59, 363).

15. Cf. the allegory of the spider as *avaro* in a sermon preached by St. Bernardine in Florence during Lent, 1425, in *Le prediche volgari inedite*, ed. D. Pacetti (Siena: Cantagalli, 1935), I, 293-315. In the revised version of the dialogue, Poggio includes a passage against this allegorical interpretation of poets (Garin, ed., *Prosatori*, p. 1129). Cf. Harth, "Niccolò Niccoli," p. 30n3.

16. The topic of old men's avarice had been discussed in Petrarch's *Secretum*, where Franciscus defended his concern over money with an argument similar to Antonio's here. See Petrarca, *Prose*, p. 88: "Senectutis pauperiem ante prospiciens si fatigate etati adiumenta conquiro, quid hic tam reprehensible est?" In *Fam.*, XX, 14, 19, Petrarch observes that old men are generally avaricious, according to Aristotle (*Rhet.* 1389a 14-16). A similar defense of money from a pessimistic viewpoint is that of Adovardo in Book III of Alberti's *Famiglia: Opere volgari*, ed. C. Grayson, I (Bari, 1960), 246-247.

17. Cicero, *De senectute*, 18, 66, a text quoted by Petrarch (*Fam.*, XIV, 4, 17; XVII, 8, 8) and paraphrased by him in his *Secretum*, pp. 86-88: "Nunc mutatis moribus, infelix, quo magis ad terminum appropinquas, eo viatici reliquum conquiris attentius."

18. Valla quotes the passage to contrast the Stoic abstractions, implicit in Cicero's context, to common usage. See his *Opera omnia*, I, 688.

19. Cf. Cicero, *De or.*, II, 28, 121; *De leg.*, I, 13, 36; *Tusc. disp.*, II, 2, 5; IV, 4, 7; *De nat. deor.*, III, 1, 1; *Lucullus*, 3, 7-8; *De div.*, II, 72, 150.

20. See Harth, "Niccolò Niccoli," pp. 51-53.

21. The notion of progress from the inception of a discipline derives from Cicero, *Brutus*, 18, 71: "nescio an reliquis in rebus omnibus idem eveniat: nihil est enim simul et inventum et perfectum." The same passage is cited in Leon Battista Alberti's *Della pittura* of 1436, *Opere volgari*, III (Bari, 1973), 106-107.

22. Cf. *De avaritia*, I, 6: "non tam disserendi causa, quam aut te aut hunc provocandi," and Cicero, *De fin.*, I, 8, 26: "Quae cum dixissem, magis ut illum provocarem quam ut ipse loquerer." In Cicero, however, the sense of the *provocatio* does not extend to his readership.

23. See Ton. I, 273; Walser, *Poggius*, p. 429.

24. Terence, *Andria*, 68: "veritas solet odium parere," also quoted by Poggio in *Contra hypocritas* (II, 51) and *De miseria humanae conditionis* (I, 100) in religious contexts.

25. On the "reversal" of traditional treatments inherent in Poggio's choice of titles, see Fubini, "Intendimenti", p. 553n52.

26. In a letter of 1455 to Andrea Alamanni, Poggio declares that reading and meditation are superior to teaching and discussion in the pursuit of eloquence, citing the examples of learned men from Petrarch to his own generation (Ton. III, 184-186).

IV. Lorenzo Valla and the Rhetorical Dialogue

Epigraph: Lorenzo Valla, *De vero falsoque bono*, ed. Maristella De Panizza Lorch (Bari: Adriatica, 1970), p. 15: "et nostris quoque temporibus licet philosophi se rectores aliorum dicant, tamen oratores, ut res ipsa docet, rectores aliorum esse ac principes quidem dicendi sunt." Unless otherwise stated, all citations for Valla refer to this edition.

1. See Mario Fois, *Il pensiero cristiano di Lorenzo Valla nel quadro storico-culturale del suo ambiente,* Analecta Gregoriana, 174 (Rome: Università Gregoriana, 1969), pp. 98-104; Franco Gaeta, *Lorenzo Valla: Filologia e storia nell'Umanesimo italiano* (Naples: Istituto italiano per gli studi storici, 1955), pp. 15-53; Jerrold E. Seigel, *Rhetoric and Philosophy in Renaissance Humanism: The Union of Eloquence and Wisdom, Petrarch to Valla* (Princeton: Princeton University Press, 1968), pp. 144-160; Charles Trinkaus, *In Our Image and Likeness: Humanity and Divinity in Italian Humanist Thought* (Chicago: University of Chicago Press, 1970), pp. 105-150; Giovanni Di Napoli, *Lorenzo Valla: Filosofia e religione nell'Umanesimo italiano* (Rome: Edizioni di storia e letteratura, 1971), pp. 177-246; Salvatore I. Camporeale, *Lorenzo Valla: Umanesimo e teologia* (Florence: Istituto Nazionale di Studi sul Rinascimento, 1972); Hanna-Barbara Gerl, *Rhetorik als Philosophie: Lorenzo Valla,* Humanistische Bibliothek, I, 13 (Munich: Wilhelm Fink, 1974), pp. 88-191; Riccardo Fubini, "Note su Lorenzo Valla e la composizione del 'De voluptate,'" in *I classici nel Medioevo e nell' Umanesimo: Miscellanea filologica,* Università di Genova, Facoltà di lettere, Istituto di filologia classica e medioevale (Genoa, 1975), pp. 11-57.

2. Antonio's *iudicium* (pp. 94-95) recalls Cicero, *De nat. deor.*, III, 40, 95: "ut Velleio Cottae disputatio verior, mihi Balbi ad veritatis similitudinem videretur esse propensior." Catone's Stoic position seems closer to the truth (p. 107): "Cato autem, cuius oratio propius ad veritatem accedere videtur," according to Antonio, who echoes another Ciceronian passage (*De or.*, I, 62, 262): "Haec cum Antonius dixisset, sane dubitare visus est Sulpicius et Cotta, utrius oratio propius ad veritatem videretur accedere." Although the influence of *De finibus* is important, Valla applies his borrowings to new contexts. Cf. Fubini, "Note," pp. 30-33.

3. On the shield of faith and the sword of the spirit, see Ephesians 6:16-17; on Jonathan and David, see I Kings 14:1-23, 17:22-54. The image of philosophers in self-destructive battle is also found in Lactantius' *De opificio Dei,* 20 (*PL,* 7, 77), and his *Divinae Institutiones,* III, 4 (*PL,* 6, 358).

4. On the concept of Lactantius as a refuter of paganism, see Jerome, Epistle 58 (*PL,* 22, 585).

5. The passage from Acts is also noted in Augustine's *Sermons* and his *City of God,* XVIII, 41. See Fubini, "Note," pp. 31-32.

6. Bruni, *Dialogus I,* p. 62; Valla, p. 22.

7. Bruni's Book I is set in Salutati's house; in Book II the interlocutors visit Roberto Rossi's garden and then sit in his portico. At the beginning of Book III of Valla's *De vero falsoque bono,* the interlocutors move from Catone Sacco's house, where they have dined, to the adjoining gardens (p. 92).

8. Poggio's Loschi reinstates the Academic method; Valla's Vegio allies himself with the Academic Carneades. Poggio's Loschi exploits a passage from Augustine to defend avarice (I, 12); Valla's Vegio denounces Regulus (pp. 45,

51-52), the classical exemplar praised in Augustine's *City of God* (e.g. I, 24).

9. Cf. Vespasiano da Bisticci, *Le Vite*, ed. A. Greco, II (Florence: Istituto Nazionale per Studi sul Rinascimento, 1976), 232: "Era Nicolaio molto morale nelle sua sententie, et sempre parlava come buono et fedele cristiano."

10. In citing the Bible, both Andreas and Antonio interpret synonyms to support their argument: Andreas equates Paul's *cupiditas* with *avaritia* (I, 27-28), and Antonio identifies the *delectatio* (Greek *tryphé*) of the Psalms with *voluptas* (p. 110).

11. Cf. Augustine, *Contra Academicos* (*PL*, 32, 918).

12. Cf. Cicero, *Tusc. disp.*, II, 2, 5.

13. Gerl, *Rhetorik*, pp. 149-173.

14. Vegio echoes Valla's Pauline sword metaphor in a rhetorical context. His preference for rhetoric over philosophy, seconded by Bripi (p. 15) and Antonio (Book III), constitutes a reversal of the polemic conducted by Lactantius against orators at the beginning of his *Divinae institutiones*, I, 1 (*PL*, 6, 114).

15. The image of defenseless man echoes Lactantius, *De opificio Dei*, 3 (*PL*, 7, 16)—a source, with Quintilian, for the commonplace of nature as stepmother. The objection to beating children ("Ista, seva, ne in pueros quidem probatur") may derive from Quintilian, *Institutio oratoria*, I, 3, 14.

16. On *ficta oratio*, see Quintilian, *Inst. orat.*, VI, 1, 23-25. Valla echoes two passages in Quintilian's subsequent account of the *miseratio:* "et producere ipsos, qui periclitentur, squalidos atque deformes et liberos eorum ac parentes" (VI, 1, 30) and "Tendit ad genua vestra supplices manus" (VI, 1, 42).

17. Cicero calls the Stoics' writings squalid, *De fin.*, IV, 3, 5.

18. Cf. the analogous moral verdict of Quintilian, XII, 1, 23: "Concedamus sane, quod minime natura patitur, repertum esse aliquem malum virum summe disertum: nihilo tamen minus oratorem eum negabo."

19. Cf. Quintilian, *Inst. orat.*, XII, 1, 1: "si vis illa dicendi malitiam instruxerit, nihil . . . publicis privatisque rebus perniciosius eloquentia."

20. *Inst. orat.*, XII, 1, 1-3: "Sit ergo nobis orator, quem constituimus, is, qui a M. Catone finitur, vir bonus dicendi peritus; verum, id quod et ille posuit prius et ipsa natura potius ac maius est, utique vir bonus . . . quod, si vis illa dicendi malitiam instruxerit, nihil sit publicis privatisque rebus perniciosius eloquentia, nosque ipsi, qui pro virili parte conferre aliquid ad facultatem dicendi conati sumus, pessime mereamur de rebus humanis, si latroni comparamus haec arma, non militi. Quid de nobis loquor? Rerum ipsa natura in eo, quod indulsisse homini videtur quoque nos a ceteris animalibus separasse, non parens, sed noverca fuerit, si facultatem dicendi, sociam scelerum, adversam innocentiae, hostem veritatis invenit . . . Neque enim tantum id dico, eum, qui sit orator, virum bonum esse oportere, sed ne futurum quidem oratorem nisi virum bonum." Valla uses the phrase "natura indulxit" repeatedly (pp. 10, 16); cf. "indulgentissima mater" (p. 17). At the beginning of the dialogue, Giovanni Marchi quotes Quintilian, XII, 1, 30: "Bonos nunquam honestus sermo deficiet, nunquam rerum optimarum" (p. 4).

21. Like Carneades, Vegio argues against justice (p. 61). On Carneades as antagonist of the Stoics, see Cicero, *De fin.*, II, 13, 42; *De nat. deor.*, II, 65, 162; III, 17, 44.

22. In his *Contra Academicos*, II, 12, 27 (*PL*, 32, 932), Augustine denounces Carneades. As late as Petrarch, the judgment of Carneades was negative. See his *Fam.*, XXII, 2, 6; *Trionfo della Fama*, III, 97-99.

23. Vegio's discussion of historical examples of *honestas* (p. 48) treats the cases of "Cato, Scipio, et preter cuntos, Lucretia" respectively, an order suggested by Quintilian's remark on *exempla*, V, 11, 10: "si ad fortiter faciendum accendatur aliquis, non tantum adferent momenti . . . ad moriendum . . . Cato et Scipio quam Lucretia."

24. *Inst. orat.*, XII, 1, 14-15: "omnia, quae in eum ab inimicis congesta sunt"; *De vero falsoque bono*, p. 91: "magis inimice quam vere obiecisse."

25. Acts of the Apostles 17:21 reads "Athenienses autem omnes, et advenae hospites, ad nihil aliud vacabant nisi aut dicere, aut audire aliquid novi." As if rivaling the apostle Paul, Valla's Antonio emphasizes the novelty of his doctrine of pleasure.

26. In his refutation of Stoic virtue, Vegio repeatedly refers to the negative "premia" which reward "honestas" (pp. 45, 46) and asserts that the motivation of virtue is a reward, or pleasure (p. 52: "Hoc dixisse satis est: universos ad preclare de patria merendum aliquo premio fuisse evocatos").

27. Gerl, *Rhetorik*, pp. 97-118.

28. Valla, *Opera omnia*, I, 688, contrasts the "actissima veritatis lex ac Stoica" and Cicero's expresson "non ad aurificis stateram sed ad popularem quandam trutinam." See also Gerl, *Rhetorik*, p. 226n129.

29. Cf. Marrou, *Saint Augustin*, pp. 368-380 and *passim*.

30. Bruni, *Humanistische-philosophische Schriften*, p. 142: "Ego tamen dicam de summo bono in quantum hominis, nam post mortem non est homo amplius."

V. Leon Battista Alberti and the Volgare Dialogue

Epigraph: Leon Battista Alberti, *Opere volgari*, ed. Cecil Grayson, I (Bari: Laterza, 1960), 305: "Ponete qui animo, Battista e tu Carlo; a voi, non a Lionardo, uomo dottissimo, repeto questi principii di mezzo le fonti de' filosofi." Unless otherwise noted, all citations for Alberti's *volgare* writings refer to this edition—vols. I (1960), II (1966), and III (1973). Cf. Cicero, *De or.*, II, 27, 118: "vobis hoc, Cotta et Sulpici, dico."

1. On Book IV of *Libri della Famiglia*, dated 1437, see R. Fubini and A. Menci Gallorini, "L'autobiografia di Leon Battista Alberti: Studio e edizione," *Rinascimento*, II, 12 (1972), 30.

2. See esp. Paul-Henri Michel, *Un idéal humain au XVe siècle: La pensée de L. B. Alberti* (Paris: Les belles lettres, 1930); Giovanni Santinello, *Leon Battista Alberti: Una visione estetica del mondo e della vita* (Florence: Sansoni, 1962); Joan Gadol, *Leon Battista Alberti: Universal Man of the Early Renaissance* (Chicago: University of Chicago Press, 1969); Cecil Grayson, "The Humanism of Alberti," *Italian Studies*, 12 (1957), 37-56; Eugenio Garin,

Rinascite e rivoluzioni: Movimenti culturali dal XIV al XVIII secolo (Bari: Laterza, 1975), pp. 131-196; Giovanni Ponte, "Leon Battista Alberti umanista e prosatore," *Rassegna della letteratura italiana*, 7 (1964), 256-85; Ponte, "Etica ed economia nel terzo libro 'Della Famiglia' di Leon Battista Alberti," in *Renaissance Studies in Honor of Hans Baron*, ed. A. Molho and J. A. Tedeschi (Florence: Sansoni, 1971), pp. 283-309; Tateo, *Tradizione*, pp. 279-318.

3. See Raffaele Spongano, "La prosa letteraria del Quattrocento," in Leon Battista Alberti, *I primi tre libri della Famiglia*, ed. F. C. Pellegrini, 2nd ed. (Florence: Sansoni, 1946), pp. vii-xxxii; Cecil Grayson, "Appunti sulla lingua dell'Alberti," *Lingua nostra*, 16 (1955), 105-110; Ghino Ghinassi, "Leon Battista Alberti fra latinismo e toscanismo: La revisione dei *Libri della Famiglia*," *Lingua nostra*, 22 (1967), 1-6; Maurizio Dardano, "Sintassi dell'infinito nei *Libri della Famiglia* di L. B. Alberti," *Annali della Scuola Normale Superiore di Pisa*, 32 (1963), 83-135; Dardano, "Sintassi e stile nei *Libri della Famiglia* di Leon Battista Alberti," *Cultura neolatina*, 23 (1963), 215-250.

4. Thus in Book IV of *Libri della Famiglia* (I, 284), Adovardo questions the use of debating about honorable friendships as opposed to useful or pleasurable friendships, a distinction of terminology fundamental to Valla's *De vero bono*.

5. See Dardano, "Sintassi e stile," p. 220.

6. Cf. Eugenio Garin, "Il pensiero di Leon Battista Alberti: Caratteri e contrasti," *Rinascimento*, II, 12 (1972), 3-20.

7. I, 87: "dove ancora piaccia essercitarti lo 'ngegno in confutare le mie e persuadere le tue ragioni, loderotti disputando, ove ancora esserciti la memoria recando a mente sentenze, autorità ed essempli, conferendo similitudini, argumenti, quali tu apresso i buoni scrittori arai trovate atte a quello di che noi ragionassimo." The debate between Lionardo and Battista suggests by its artificial tone the influence of contemporary humanist dialogues. Whereas the praise of mental exercise is Brunian, Lionardo's allusion to finding examples and comparing similes recalls the powers of the orator cited by Antonio in Valla, *De vero falsoque bono*, p. 113.

8. I, 261 (Giannozzo): "siate giusti, veritieri e massai. Così sarete fortunati, amati e onorati"; I, 22 (Lorenzo): "di certo niuno sarà maggior conforto a' vecchi quanto . . . vederli [*sc.* i giovani] per loro costumi e virtù esser pregiati, amati e onorati."

9. As Crassus urges Cotta and Sulpicius to continue their studies (*De or.*, I, 8, 34), so Lionardo urges Battista and Carlo (I, 69, 128). Sulpicius in turn welcomes Crassus' discourse by exclaiming "o diem . . . nobis . . . optatum!" (*De or.*, I, 30, 136), while Battista greets Lionardo's remarks with the Latin exclamation "O diem utilissimam!" (I, 128).

10. Lorenzo says that he usually remained standing in the presence of his elders, the proper behavior depicted by Alberti in *Libri della Famiglia* (I, 166) and *De Iciarchia* (II, 188). For the Quattrocento custom of youths standing around seated elders, see also Bruni, *Dialogus II*, p. 76; Matteo Palmieri, *Vita civile*, ed. F. Battaglia (Bologna: Zanichelli, 1944), p. 112.

11. Cf. *De senectute* 6, 17-20. In *De senectute,* Alberti also found extended praise of villa life (15, 51) and an exhortation to read Xenophon's *Oeconomicus* (17, 59).

12. On the resemblance of Alberti's "Battista e tu Carlo" (I, 305, and *passim*) to Cicero's "C. Fanni et tu Q. Muci" (*De amicitia,* 27, 100), see L. B. Alberti, *I primi tre libri della Famiglia,* ed. F. C. Pellegrini (Florence: Sansoni, 1911), p. 143; Michel, *Un idéal humain,* p. 120n3.

13. *De am.*, 9, 32: "(Laelius) Ortum quidem amicitiae videtis, nisi quod ad haec forte vultis. (Fannius) Tu vero perge Laeli; pro hoc enim qui minor est natu, meo iure respondeo. (Scaevola) Recte tu quidem. Quam ob rem audiamus. (Laelius) Audite vero optumi viri." Alberti, I, 103: "(Battista) Tu continua el dir tuo. Noi t'ascolteremo. (Lionardo) Piacemi. Così faremo . . . Ascoltatemi." This hortatory "Listen" is a common feature in *De Iciarchia* as well, where the aged Battista addresses the youths, "Udite, giovani" (II, 229).

14. Alberti, *De commodis,* ed. Goggi Carotti, pp. 46-47.

15. On *mediocrità* as a moral ideal, see *De Iciarchia,* II, 189; Santinello, *Una visione estetica,* p. 185. The notion of a conversation of moderate learning, intended for neither the ignorant nor the erudite, is formulated (with a citation from Lucilius) by Crassus in Cicero, *De or.*, II, 6, 25, a passage which no doubt influenced Alberti's concept of the *ragionamento domestico.*

16. "A' dotti potrei io se non dire cose a loro notissime; gl'ignoranti, stimate, di me e di mie sentenze poco farebbono giudicio, poco conto. Quelli vero che sono alquanto tinti di lettere, vorrebbono udire in me quella prisca eloquenza elimatissima e suavissima." Cf. Adovardo in Book IV, I, 301: "Niuno sarà ancora tinto di lettere, che me non riprenda arrogante e non contento della dottrina e scritti de' maggiori, tanta età da tutti approvati." The phrase "tinto di lettere" derives from Cicero, *De or.*, II, 20, 85 ("tinctus litteris").

17. I, 84: "Quasi, Battista, come se a te non stessi a mente la sentenza del tuo Marco Cicerone, el quale tu suoli tanto lodare e amare, che giudica nessuna cosa essere più flessibile e duttibile quanto la orazione. Questa segue e viene dovunque tu la volgi e guidi, né il ragionare nostro, el quale come vedi è tra noi domestico, si richiede essere gastigato ed emendato quanto quello de' filosofi nelle loro oscurissime e difficillime questioni, e' quali disputando seguono ogni minimo membro, e della materia lasciano adrieto nulla non bene esplicato e molto aperto. Tra noi el nostro ragionare non cerca laude d'ingegno, né ammirazione di eloquenza." Battista's wonder at the number of topics emphasizes the free course of the discussion. Alberti's interlocutors repeatedly observe that they do not know how a certain topic has arisen (I, 61, 105, 299), a Ciceronian trait common in the Quattrocento dialogue. See Tateo, *Tradizione,* p. 236.

18. Thus Santinello (*Una visione estetica,* p. 135) complains that the uncontrolled torrent of precepts and examples in Alberti's middle dialogues—*Libri della Famiglia IV, Theogenius,* and *Profugiorum*—seems designed to bore the reader.

19. On Alberti's frequent recourse to similes, see Ponte, "L. B. Alberti

umanista e prosatore," p. 272n69. Alberti calls attention to this predilection when writing to Paolo Codagnello in *De amore*, III, 259: "Sai troppo a me piace addurre scrivendo qualche similitudine." He also uses similes in his technical writings, as in *De pictura*, III, 30: "E per meglio intendere questo, useremo una similitudine."

20. R. Romano and A. Tenenti, editors of the Einaudi edition of *Libri della Famiglia* (Turin, 1969), identify Lionardo's diffidence with the feelings of Alberti himself in revising his dialogue (p. 122n17).

21. See Alberti, *I primi tre libri della Famiglia*, ed. Pellegrini (1911), pp. xxxii-xxxiv; Michel, *Un idéal humain*, pp. 188-189; Santinello, *Una visione estetica*, pp. 13-14, 135, 259.

22. "E quinci nacque come e' dicono: *Nihil dictum quin prius dictum*. E veggonsi queste cose litterarie usurpate da tanti, e in tanti loro scritti adoperate e disseminate, che oggi a chi voglia ragionarne resta altro nulla che solo el raccogliere e assortirle e poi accoppiarle insieme con qualche varietà dagli altri e adattezza dell'opera sua, quasi come suo instituto sia imitare in questo chi altrove fece el pavimento." On Alberti's citing the Terentian dictum (*Eunuch*, 41), see Santinello, *Una visione estetica*, p. 33n8.

23. Niccola's reference to the "industria e diligenza" of Agnolo recalls Alberti's description of his own industry and diligence in the prologue to *Libri della Famiglia* (I, 12). The gratitude of Niccola was not shared by the Alberti family; in *Profugiorum* Alberti wished to thank himself.

24. Cf. Santinello, *Una visione estetica*, pp. 13-14, 135, 259.

25. Grayson, "The Humanism of Alberti," p. 55, notes the incompleteness of Alberti's moral and literary works and the harmony of his practical and artistic works. Aware of his literary shortcomings (Terence's "Nihil dictum quin prius dictum"), Alberti sought in the simile of the mosaic the originality and perfection of design that he realized in his practical and artistic works.

26. Paraphrasing Cicero's *Brutus* (18, 71) at the end of his *De pictura*, (III, 106, 107) Alberti observes that nothing is at once invented and perfected, and he exhorts his readers to improve on his initial effort. On Alberti's sense of the novelty of Florentine art as expressed in his dedicatory letter to Brunelleschi (III, 7-8), see Hans Baron, "The *Querelle* of the Ancients and the Moderns," in *Renaissance Essays*, ed. P. O. Kristeller and P. P. Wiener (New York: Harper Torchbooks, 1968), p. 111.

27. I, 87: "se io forse dicessi cosa da voi dottissimi non lodata, dirolla non tanto perché a me paia dire il vero, quanto per essercitarmi." Lionardo had already encouraged Battista by asserting that any position may be sustained for the contrast of debate, I, 87: "per conferire sempre fu licito difendere qualunque opinione per falso ch'ella fusse."

28. On the leisurely nature of Cicero's discussions, see Becker, *Technik und Szenerie*, p. 56.

29. See Bec, *Les marchands ecrivains*, pp. 316-415; Lauro Marines, *The Social World of the Florentine Humanists, 1390-1460* (Princeton: Princeton University Press, 1963), pp. 31-32.

30. Alberti, *De commodis,* ed. Goggi Carotti, pp. 101-106. Cf. Alberti, *Scriptor,* in *Opera inedita,* p. 125.

31. Fubini and Menci Gallorini, "L'autobiografia," pp. 71-72: "Cum libros *De familia* primum, secundum atque tertium suis legendos tradidisset, aegre tulit eos inter omnes Albertos, alioquin ociosissimos, vix unum repertum fore, qui titulos librorum perlegere dignatus sit."

32. Fubini and Menci Gallorini, "L'autobiografia," p. 70: "brevi tempore multo suo studio, multa industria id assecutus extitit, ut sui cives, qui in senatu se dici eloquentes cuperent, non paucissima ex illius scriptis ad exornandam orationem suam ornamenta in dies suscepisse faterentur"; p. 72: "Illis libris illecti, plerique rudes concives studiosissimi litterarum effecti sunt. Eos caeterosque omnes cupidos litterarum fratrum loco deputabat."

33. *De commodis,* ed. Goggi Carotti, pp. 104-105.

34. *De Iciarchia,* II, 214-215. Cf. Martines, *Social World,* pp. 296-297.

35. Martines, *Social World,* p. 63.

36. Cicero, *Brutus,* 16, 62: "ad memoriam laudum domesticarum et ad illustrandam nobilitatem suam." See also Fubini and Menci Gallorini, "L'autobiografia," p. 27.

VI. Giovanni Pontano and the Academic Gathering

Epigraph: Giovanni Pontano, *I Dialoghi,* ed. C. Previtera (Florence: Sansoni, 1943), p. 280: "quanquam senem me annisque gravatum, spes tamen cepit fore ut, antequam a vobis emigrem, Latinam videam philosophiam et cultu maiore verborum et elegantia res suas explicantem utque, relicta litigatrice hac disputandi ratione, quietiorem ipsa formam accipiat et dicendi et sermocinandi ac verbis item suis utendi propriis maximeque Romanis." All citations for Pontano's dialogues refer to this edition.

1. See Francesco Tateo, *L'umanesimo etico di Giovanni Pontano* (Lecce: Milella, 1972), pp. 11-120, 189-210; Tateo, *Tradizione,* pp. 319-354; S. Mariotti, "Per lo studio dei dialoghi del Pontano," *Belfagor,* 2 (1947), 332-344; Giuseppe Toffanin, *Giovanni Pontano fra l'uomo e natura* (Bologna: Zanichelli, 1938); S. Monti, "L'apografo corsiniano dell' 'Aegidius' di Gioviano Pontano," *Rendiconti dell'Accademia di Archeologia, Lettere e Belle Arti di Napoli,* 44 (1969), 243-258.

2. On the dating of Pontano's dialogues, see S. Monti, "Ricerche sulla cronologia dei 'Dialoghi' del Pontano," *Annali della Facoltà di Lettere e Filosofia dell'Università di Napoli,* 10 (1962-1963), 254-276. Lucianic features in *Charon* and *Antonius* include the description of various nations or cities (as in Lucian's *De sacrificiis*), the use of laws and archaic legal language (*Timon, Menippus*), and the grammarians' duel (*Soloecista*).

3. The opening of *Charon* echoes Cicero's *De officiis,* III, 1, 1. On Lucian's conscious blend of philosophy and comedy (*Prometheus es,* 6), see Hirzel, *Der Dialog,* II, 274-275.

4. Cf. Mariotti, "Per lo studio," pp. 338: "l'Asinus . . . è sostanzialmente il lungo prologo di una conversazione scientifica, sulla cui

soglia lo scrittore ha deposto la penna. All'arrivo ufficiale dei suoi interlocutori l'opera d'arte era ormai compiuta."

5. See e.g. Tateo, *L'umanesimo etico*, pp. 200-210; John W. O'Malley, *Giles of Viterbo on Church and Reform: A Study in Renaissance Thought*, Studies in Medieval and Reformation Thought, 5 (Leiden: Brill, 1968).

6. Pontano greets the arrival of Pucci and Tamira on their customary ("de more") visit to the Academy (p. 255), and later Tamira notes that others have joined the group (p. 260).

7. P. 260 (Tamira): "nos, o Pucci, ita quidem consessionis huius memores esse oportet, ut quae Porticus ipsius lex est, eam cum primis sequamur, quippe cum disserendi locus suus sit cuique relinquendus." Cf. *Actius*, pp. 203, 231.

8. The affinities with *Phaedo* are striking. The visitors Suardino and Peto recall the Thebans Cebes and Simmias in Plato's dialogue, and Pontano's association of his Latin philosophy with the "Christian Muses" suggests Socrates' identification of music with philosophy (*Phaedo*, 61 A). The valedictory tone of the two works is similar, and Pontano's hope for the future (p. 280)—shared by Pucci and Tamira—recalls Socrates' farewell in *Apology* (40 C). Cf. Cicero's translation of Plato in *Tusc. disp.*, I, 41, 97: "magna me . . . spes tenet," and Tamira in *Aegidius*, p. 260: "Magna et me . . . spes tenet."

9. The alternation of serious discussion and lighter scenes creates a generally symmetrical structure usually reinforced by verbal and thematic links between corresponding sections, as in the three principal discussions of *Charon* (pp. 6, 27, 43). Pontano often calls attention at the end of a dialogue to its initial topic (*Actius*, p. 239; *Aegidius*, p. 279).

10. Pontano's allusion to Altilio (p. 266) is echoed by Summonte, p. 268: "ut a quo tua, Ioviane, coepit, ad eundem quoque Altilium mea convertatur oratio." The centrality of this passage is established in Pontano's first draft of *Aegidius*, written before Calenzio's death; in that version, an obscure young poet ("Dionysius") is lamented in the same terms as Calenzio. See Monti, "L'apografo corsiniano," pp. 249-253.

11. Sannazaro's allusion to the Sirens and Muses recalls the opening scene (pp. 247-248), while the evocation of his garden suggests the gardens of Pontano's villa (p. 248) and the monastery gardens (p. 280) in which Giles addressed his friends. Sannazaro's departure "animo vultuque quam maxime hilari" (p. 268) recalls the appearance of Ferrando Gennaro in *Actius*, p. 132: "vultu iucundus, risu hilaris." The passages are also linked by the repeated theme of *desiderium*. Cf. *Actius*, pp. 132-133.

12. Pontano and Summonte both recognize the need to moderate their *desiderium* (p. 267) for Sannazaro. Calenzio has likewise left behind him a *desiderabilem memoriam* (p. 268).

13. Cf. *Aegidius*, p. 266; Lorenzo Valla, *De vero falsoque bono*, pp. 127-129.

14. Cf. Erasmus, *Ausgewählte Schriften*, ed. W. Welzig, VI (Darmstadt: Wissenschaftliche Buchgesellschaft, 1967), 30-36.

15. On Valla and Pontano, see David Marsh, "Grammar, Method, and Polemic in Lorenzo Valla's *Elegantiae*," *Rinascimento*, II, 19 (1979), in press.

16. The noun *habilitas* proposed by Pontano is found in Cicero, *De legibus*, I, 9, 27, in a discussion of man's natural gifts.

17. The phrase echoes Cicero, *De legibus*, I, 3, 9: *subsiciva tempora*, "odd hours"—originally an agricultural term.

18. See Poggio, *De nobilitate*, I, 66-70.

19. See Erasmus, *Opus epistolarum*, II, 99; Tateo, *Tradizione*, p. 251n1. Erasmus was perhaps familiar only with Pontano's *Charon* and *Antonius*, the most Lucianic dialogues, for in his *Ciceronianus*, Bulephorus says of Pontano that besides certain moral tracts "non memini me quicquam illius legisse praeter aliquot dialogos ad Lucianum effictos," Erasmus, *Ausgewählte Schriften*, ed. W. Welzig, VII (Darmstadt: Wissenschaftliche Buchgesellschaft, 1972), 316.

20. P. 193: "quo e priscis vel consultore utar vel auctore? . . . innuens quidem, ut tu ipse, Puderice, exigis, potius quam praecipiens, dicam de historia aliquid." Cf. pp. 209, 213, 225, 230.

21. P. 230: "Et promissis a te satisfactum, Altili, confitemur omnes et disserendis iis incredibili voluptate nos affecisti, dum rem sparsam ac passim iactatam colligis collectamque ordine suo suaque regula ac lege sic componis, ut si qui posthac redacturi ea sint in praecepta, facile quidem praestituri id videantur."

22. Giovanni Pontano, *De sermone libri sex*, ed. S. Lupi and A. Risicato (Lugano: Thesaurus mundi, 1954), provides a social theory of language, as Pontano's *De aspiratione* examines grammatical questions at the minute level of orthography.

23. The disquisitions of Guarino Veronese in Angelo Decembrio, *Politia litteraria* (Augsburg, 1540) are another example of a generally grammatical symposium.

24. See Monti, "Ricerche sulla cronologia," pp. 254-276.

25. Although Alberti's dialogues reflect the conflicts of his character, the autobiographical detail of Pontano's dialogues is unique. See C. M. Tallarigo, *Giovanni Pontano e i suoi tempi* (Naples, 1874): E. Percopo, "La vita di Giovanni Pontano," *Archivio storico per le Province Napoletane*, 61 (1936), 116-250.

26. The lapidary inscription (p. 245) and Pardo's citing of Pontano as an example of ancient virtue (p. 277) contribute to Pontano's stature as an ideal figure in *Aegidius*.

27. The image of barking or rabid whelps pervades *Antonius* (pp. 58-59, 61-62, 66, 78, 82).

28. *Antonius*, p. 57: "civitas nostra tota delirum est."

29. *Charon*, p. 27: "sermo hic qui de superstitione est."

30. P. 259: "Iniquitate temporum factum est plurimis ut etiam seculis dicendi laus a disciplinarum cognitione seiuncta fuerit, cum antea quidem nemo doctus quin idem quoque esset eloquens. Sed eloquentiae studium post Romani imperii declinationem Prorsus interiit vixque grammaticae ipsius

perstitere vestigia, cum tamen disciplinae ipsae in honore essent habitae, id quod physicorum theologorumque multitudo quae post Boetium extitit plane declarat, tum in Hispania, tum in Galliis Britanniisque ipsaque in Germania." For "iniquitas temporum," see also p. 280 and *Actius*, p. 231, as well as "temporum vitium" in Bruni, *Dialogus I*, p. 60.

31. P. 259: "Nos quidem, bone Senex, oratio haec tua quam oraculum ipsum non minus incendere ad dicendi frugem ad quam ipse hortaris iure suo potest."

Index

Harvard Studies in Comparative Literature

1 *Three Philosophical Poets: Lucretius, Dante, and Goethe.* By George Santayana. 1910
2 *Chivalry in English Literature: Chaucer, Malory, Spenser, and Shakespeare.* By William Henry Schofield. 1912
3 *The Comedies of Holberg.* By Oscar James Campbell, Jr. 1914
4 *Medieval Spanish Allegory.* By Chandler Rathfon Post. 1915
5 *Mythical Bards and the Life of William Wallace.* By William Henry Schofield. 1920
6 *Angevin Britain and Scandinavia.* By Henry Goddard Leach. 1921
7 *Chaucer and the Roman Poets.* By Edgar Finley Shannon. 1929
8 *Spenser and the Table Round.* By Charles Bowie Millican. 1932
9 *Eger and Grime.* By James Ralston Caldwell. 1933
10 *Virgil the Necromancer.* By John Webster Spargo. 1934
11 *Chaucer's Use of Proverbs.* By Bartlett Jere Whiting. 1934
12 *English Literature and Culture in Russia (1553-1840).* By Ernest J. Simmons. 1935
13 *D'Edmond Spenser à Alan Seeger: Poèmes Anglais Traduits en Vers Français.* By Fernand Baldensperger. 1938
14 *Proverbs in the Earlier English Drama.* By Bartlett Jere Whiting. 1938
15 *Catullus in Strange and Distant Britain.* By James A. S. McPeek. 1939
16 *Jean Racine.* By Alexander F. B. Clark. 1939
17 *Un Voyageur-Philosophe au XVIII Siècle: L'Abbé Jean-Bernard le Blanc.* By Hélène Monod-Cassidy. 1941
18 *A Bibliography of the Theophrastan Character in English with Several Portrait Characters.* By Chester Noyes Greenough and J. M. French. 1947
19 *The Testament of Werther in Poetry and Drama.* By Stuart Pratt Atkins. 1949
20 *Perspectives of Criticism.* Edited by Harry Levin. 1950
21 *Vissarion Belinski, 1811-1848.* By Herbert E. Bowman. 1954
22 *Contexts of Criticism.* By Harry Levin. 1957
23 *On Translation.* Edited by Reuben A. Brower. 1959
24 *The Singer of Tales.* By Albert B. Lord. 1960
25 *Praisers of Folly: Erasmus, Rabelais, Shakespeare.* By Walter Kaiser. 1963
26 *Rogue's Progress: Studies in the Picaresque Novel.* By Robert Alter. 1964

27 *Dostoevsky and Romantic Realism: A Study of Dostoevsky in Relation to Balzac, Dickens, and Gogol.* By Donald Fanger. 1965
28 *The Icelandic Family Saga: An Analytic Reading.* By Theodore M. Andersson. 1967
29 *Roman Laughter: The Comedy of Plautus.* By Erich Segal. 1968
30 *Pan the Goat God: His Myth in Modern Times.* By Patricia Merivale. 1969
31 *The Renaissance Discovery of Time.* By Ricardo J. Quinones. 1972
32 *Grounds for Comparison.* By Harry Levin. 1972
33 *Comparative Studies in Greek and Indic Meter.* By Gregory Nagy. 1974
34 *Mirror on Mirror: Translation, Imitation, Parody.* By Reuben Brower. 1974
35 *The Quattrocento Dialogue: Classical Tradition and Humanist Innovation.* By David Marsh. 1980